KHĀKHARĀ TEMPLES

KHĀKHARĀ TEMPLES

Sanjaya Kumar Mahapatra

SHARADA

SHARADA PUBLISHING HOUSE

DELHI

First Published 2016

ISBN: 978-93-83221-13-4
₹ 2250

Published by
Anjana Bansal
SHARADA PUBLISHING HOUSE
111, Vidya Vihar Apartment
Sector-9, Rohini, Delhi-110 085 (INDIA)
Ph.: +91-11-3292 1560, 2755 2102
E-mail : bansal_sph@rediffmail.com
books@sharadabooks.com
Website : www.sharadabooks.com

Printed at

Salasar Imaging System
Delhi

Dedicated to
My Revered Gurudeva
Sri Sri Paramahamsa Hariharananda Giri
Kriya Yogi

Contents

Preface

The temples in India are closely entwined with Indian culture. They cover a plethora of interest covering art, architecture, sculpture, religious faith and rituals. Primarily temples were a place of worship of one deity or the other. But in course of time they grew into big institutions as centers of religious congregations which fostered a fraternity as it were, of the people of different hues and views. Even the dispensation of justice was done in temples. The feeling and the belief that the benign presence of god would lead the people on the right path, was at back of this phenomenon. As such, the temples of India play a vital role for the upliftment of the society and pave the way for the divinization of the people so that the materialistic world is gradually transformed to the spiritual world where everyone realizes the entity of the Supreme Absolute.

From a simple concept of worshipping an idol with water and flowers, the mode of worship gradually grew into elaborate system including varieties of *abhiṣeka, alaṅkāra* and *naivedaya* and offering various types services like recitation, dance, music and the like. Along with the growth of this concept the physical size of the temple also increased. To the *garbhagṛha,* the nucleus of the temple, came to be added several adjuncts depending upon the local needs, such as *mukhaśālā, naṭamaṇḍapa, bhōgamaṇḍapa* and the like which consisted of halls specious enough to offer different services and to accommodate the devotees gathered to witness such services. These services which consisted of various items have been very wisely condensed into two terms called *aṅgabhōga* and *raṅgabhōga. Aṅgabhōga* meant the worship of the idol through different types of anointing i.e., *abhiṣeka*, decorating the idol with flowers and different types of ornaments i.e., *alaṅkāra* and offering delicate dishes i.e., *naivedaya. Raṅgabhōga* consisted of the services offered before the god in the *raṅgamaṇḍapa* which included recitation of scriptures, songs in praise of god and dancing to please the deity.

Monuments, whether in the form of building, pillar or statue of historical importance are treated as principal visible and material records of human evolution through the ages. In India man's ideals have found expression in numerous beautiful monuments showing that few countries possess a richer architectural heritage of this kind. When we study human efforts towards building temples, forts and palaces, we find the continuous attempt of human being to express their social and religious environment and aesthetic sense through the different expression of Indian architecture, the highest achievement beyond doubt is seen in the temple, where the good is believed to reside.

It is true that temples in some form must have originated as soon as the image worship came into vogue basing upon the idea that god has made man out of his own form. When god was universally conceived in human form, such an anthropomorphic form required a habitation, a shelter and this probably resulted in preparing a structural shrine. Each and every component in a temple has a definite identity and in turn each part is a part of the whole, which is also conceived as a cosmic being or *vāstu-puruṣa.*

The temple architecture in India had its humble beginning right from the Mauryan period (third century BCE) as evident from the excavated temples at Sāñchī and Bairat. However, it gained momentum in the Gupta period. The Hindu temple was considered as one of the decisive innovations of the imperial Guptas. A large number of temples of a wide range of variety were constructed in India during the post Gupta period over a time span of more than a millennium. Geomorphologic distribution and architectural styles reveal that the temples in India can be divided into three broad groups such as *nāgara, draviḍa* and *vesara.* However, an inscription of 1215 CE in the *mukhamaṇḍapa* of the Amṛteśvara temple at Holal in Bellary district of Karnataka speaks of a fourth style, i.e. 'Kaliṅga' in addition to the former styles. Thus, it is evident that Kaliṅga, the ancient name of Orissa had a distinct position in the field of temple building India.

Situated on the east coast of India, on the Bay of Bengal, Orissa has been swept away by different religious faiths like Buddhism, Jainism, Śaivism, Vaiṣṇavism and Śaktism. The culture of Orissa has to be analyzed from the point of view of religious faiths which have passed over the region and ultimately have taken a definite shape. It may be noted that various cults and religious faiths in Orissa overlapping one another in the course of about a thousand years developed but curiously enough all these faiths have been epitomized to Jagannātha who throughout the ages has been the centre of religious life in Orissa.

Orissa is known for its rich heritage of art and architecture. Besides the rock-art of the primitive people, the earliest specimen of art of the historic period is the forepart of an elephant on rock at Dhauli near Bhubaneswar where Aśokan edicts of third century BCE have been engraved. Hindu temples constitute a major part of the architectural wealth of Orissa. The temples were built from the early sixth century to the thirteenth-fourteenth centuries when Orissa was successively ruled by the Śailodbhavas of Koṅgoḍa, Bhauma-karas of Toshala/ Utkala, Somavaṁśīs of Dakṣiṇa Kaliṅga/Orissa and the Sūryavaṁśī Gajapatis of Orissa. James Fergusson aptly remarked, "There are more temples now in Orissa than in all the rest of Hindustan put together". The architects of Orissa had several canonical texts to guide them in their planning and execution of temples. Some of the important texts which have come to lime light are *Bhuvanapradīpa, Bhuvanapraveśa, Śilpipothī, Śilpa śāstras, Saudhikāgama, Vāstu Sūtra Upaniṣad, Śilpa Sāriṇī* or *Śilpa Prakāśa, Baya Chakada* and *Padma kesara deula Mapagunnagara,* etc. The Orissan temple style did not represent a fixed type. In course of its evolution, as the building tradition was handed down from one generation to another, some changes are obvious. But in spite of the stylistic change that distinguishes one phase from another, we find a remarkable continuity in the development of the style till it reaches the climax. In course of evolution the temple architecture has been divided into five phases corresponding to the five principal dynasties that ruled Orissa from the sixth century CE to the sixteenth century CE.

The *Śilpa* texts of Orissa prescribe three types of temples such as *rekhā, pīḍhā* and *khākharā*. The *rekhā* and *pīḍhā* temples form two component parts of the same architectural scheme, the former represented by sanctum with its curvilinear spire and the latter represented by the porch having pyramidal roof made of *pīḍhā* or succeeding tiers. The *khākharā* order is noted for its semi-cylindrical roof. While the *rekhā* and *pīḍhā deula* are dedicated to Śaiva and Vaiṣṇava deities *khākharā deula* is exclusive for enshrining the Śākta divinities. Another important variation in architectural style is the hypaethral temples meant for *yoginī* cult, which however finds no mention in any *Śilpa śāstras*. During the first three centuries of the temple building activities, i.e. from sixth century to ninth century CE, it was either a circular or *khākharā* structure that enshrined the Śākta deities. In terms of antiquity the circular shrines predate the *khākharā* ones.

The present study deals with the distinct nature of the *khākharā* temples showing the marked differences with the other monuments. The generalization and characteristics have been drawn on the basis of architectural and comparative studies. The survey has brought to lime light rare but important *khākharā* temples of Orissa which glorifies the art-tradition of India.

This precious book is comprised of five chapters. First chapter, the introductory chapter deals with the cultural history of Orissa. It provides a brief sketch about the assimilation of Āryan and non-Āryan culture, growth of Jainism, Buddhism, Śaivism and Vaiṣṇavism, etc. in the land of Orissa and how all these religious faiths are absorbed in the cult of Jagannātha losing their separate entity.

Second chapter contains the Indian temples, their significance, merits gained by the temple-building activities and the various types of temples which enrich the culture of India by glorifying the art, architecture and sculpture of our subcontinent.

Third chapter throws light on the general features of Orissan temples, classification of the temples along with their components. It also focuses on the cult images and sculptures which are displayed in the temple shrines.

Fourth chapter reveals the temple building activities starting from the Śailodbhava period to the Gajapati period and after. It also contains the characteristics of the temple architecture erected during the five principal dynastical rules.

Fifth chapter forms the core of the research work, where a humble attempt has been made to survey and document, the extant *khākharā* temples of Orissa. It not only discusses the various components of the temples but also sheds light on the interpretation of these shrines and cult images according to the chronological order.

Sixth chapter concludes the above discussion and highlights the uniqueness of the *khākharā* temples of Orissa. It reveals that these temples constitute an exclusive temple type meant for the female divinity and above all this concluding chapter describes the greatness of the *khākharā* temples which enriches the art heritage of Orissa in particular and India in general.

Acknowledgements

During the course of the last two decades in which the present work moved from conception to conclusion, many people have contributed to its accomplishment. It is my first and foremost duty to express a word of appreciation to those glorified personalities without whose able guidance the present work which is so vast and versatile, could not have been completed. I fail to select words to compliment this acknowledgement to Dr Prof. Sadasiba Pradhan, Utkal University who has made the work colourful and alive by extending his help for planning, shaping and finishing it to acquire its present form and to enable it to fulfill a historical necessity.

I owe to my revered teachers and spiritual guide such as Dr Maheswar Khadanga, Reader (retd.) K.B.D.A.V. College, Nirakarpur, (Late) Pandit Sri Balabhadra Mahapatra, Sanskrit teacher, (Late) Pandit Samanta Vasudeva Mahapatra, Kulacharya, Sri Viswanath Ratha, Head Master (retd.) and Swami Yogeswaranda Giri, Kriya Yogi, Karar Ashram, Puri without whose blessings and goodwill this task would not have been a successful one. Furthermore, I am very much grateful to late Dr K.S. Behera, Senior Professor of History and (Late) Dr U.N. Dhal, Reader in Sanskrit, Dr A.N. Parida, Reader in History Department, Utkal University who have helped me a lot for the completion of the present treatise.

I am obliged to the H.O.D. Professor Dr Ashok Kumar Patnaik, Dr Sanjay Acharya, Reader and Dr Jayanti Dora, Reader along with the faculty members of the

Department of History and the Department of Ancient Indian History, Culture and Archaeology, Utkal University for their suggestions and ungrudging help.

The Chief Librarian and the staff of the Parija Library, Utkal University Bhubaneswar; the staff members of the H.K. Mahatab, State Library, Bhubaneswar; Library, P.G. Department of History, Utkal University, Library, P.G. Department of Ancient Indian History, Culture and Archaeology, Vani Vihar, Utkal University; the Orissa State Museum, Bhubaneswar; the Archaeological Survey of India, Bhubaneswar Circle; the Department of State Archaeology, Bhubaneswar, have been greatly helpful to me in providing access to all requisite data, information and records I needed. I am extremely grateful to the authorities of all these institutions. Moreover, I am extremely grateful to the Superintendent Orissa State Museum, Superintendent State Archives Bhubaneswar for library facilities.

During the course of collection of valuable materials such as photographs, palmleaf manuscripts and other relevant information I met several resourceful persons. The number is so large that it is difficult to name them all. But I am extremely grateful to them and especially I offer my thanks to Dr B.K. Rath, Former Superintendent, Department of State Archaeology, Dr C.B. Patel, Superintendent, State Museum, Bhubaneswar, Dr H.C. Das, Superintendent (retd.) Orissa State Museum, Dr Prabhash Singh, Asst. Curator, Orissa State Museum, Bhubaneswar who have helped me immensely.

I acknowledge my indebtedness to the writers whose books I have consulted and from which I have taken not only materials but also drawn illustrations. The first and foremost is the book *Orissa State Gazetteer* edited by Shri Nrusinha Charan Behuria. The second major book is the *Sakta Monuments of Orissa* authored by Dr Jayanti Dora. The third major book is the *Temples of Orissa* by Prof. Karuna Sagara Behera. The fourth major work is the *Elements of Indian Art* by S.P. Gupta and the fifth major work is the *Tantra and Sakta Art of Orissa* authored by Prof. Donaldson.

I render due reverence to my parents, elderly persons and accord my special thanks to my family members, wife and colleagues for their wise counsel, constant support and encouragement in many ways through the years for the completion of the present work.

I extend my sincere thanks to Sri Mrutyunjay Palai, Developer (.net) for completing the computer typing of the manuscript. I am also thankful to the present publisher who has extended his help for completion of the book in time.

Lastly, with steadfastness of devotion I bow my head at the lotus-feet of the Divine Mother without whose benign grace and blessings the present work would not have been accomplished.

List of Abbreviations

A.A.	*Artibus Asiatique*
A.D.	Anno Domini
A.P	Andhra Pradesh
A.S.I.	Archeological Survey of India
ASIAR	Archaeological Survey of India Annual Report
C.P.	Copper Plate
Ch.	Chapter
DBP	*Devī Bhāgavata Purāṇa*
DM	*Devī Māhātmya*
DP	*Devī Purāṇa*
e.g.	Example Gratia
E.I.	*Epigraphica India*
Ed.	Edited By
Eds.	Editors
Fig.	Figure

i.e.	That is
I.H.Q.	*Indian Historical Quarterly*
Ibid	in the same place (ibidem)
J.A.H.R.S.	*Journal of the Andhra Historical Research Society*
J.A.S.B.	*Journal of the Asiatic Society of Bengal*
J.B.O.R.S.	*Journal of Bihar and Orissa Research Society*
J.I.H.	*Journal of Indian History*
M.P.	Madhya Pradesh
MASI	Memoir of Archaeological Survey of India
Mbh	*Mahābhārata*
N.A.H.O.	New Aspects on History of Orissa
No.	Number
O.H.R.J.	*Orissa Historical Research Journal*, Bhubaneswar
O.U.P.	Oxford University Press
Op. cit.	The work cited (*opere citato*)
P.	Page
P.I.H.C.	Proceeding of Indian History Congress
pp.	Pages
RV	*Ṛgveda*
Tr	Translated by
Viz.	Namely
Vol.	Volume

List of Illustrations

List of Maps

List of Figures

List of Plates

Chapter I

Introduction

History of Orissa, which acquired indelible fame and glory under its past names such as Kaliṅga[1], Utkala[2], Udra and Oḍḍīyāna, etc. as evidenced from the ancient literature, dates back to very remote antiquity. The human history in Odisha (formerly Orissa) begins in the Lower Paleolithic Era, as Acheulian tools dating to the period have been discovered in various places in the region[3]. The State was known, far and wide, for the high cultural heritage, religious synthesis, heroic deeds, maritime trade and overseas expansion of its people. They were pioneer founders of Indian colonies across the oceans. Splendid glimpses of its remarkable past are found in many epics including *Mahābhārata.* Buddhist and Jain literature also have rich descriptions of bravery, patriotism and generosity of the people of ancient Kaliṅga. It is the soil of Orissa and supremely courageous sacrifices of its people that turned a merciless, atrocious, and barbaric *Chandaśoka* to *Dharmaśoka* amid the Kaliṅga war in 261 BCE. It is here in this soil; Aśoka abandoned his expansionism and war adventures, took asylum in Buddhism and ultimately became its great defender and propagator.

Cultural History

Culture is a word involving a number of concepts which are of greatest importance to the modern man. It is very difficult to define culture. Arnold Toynbee in his *Study of History* rejects the theory that cultural development has been due either to some superior biological instance or to a particularly easy geographical environment. Examining twenty one civilized societies within the last six thousand years while many emerged as response to challenge of nature such as drying up grassy land, silting of water source, etc., and also of massive invasion of other societies only six emerged directly from the primitive life. He has sought for an explanation of this emergence in the realm of mythology as the enshrinement of human wisdom. Perhaps this is the case in regard to Orissa. Whatever the scholars may say about culture, in the final analysis it centres round the traditional faith in one or the other region. The culture of Orissa has to be analysed from the point of view of religious faiths which have passed over the region and ultimately have taken a definite shape. For this purpose history of various religious faiths which have passed over the region have to be analysed.

Orissa as it is today consists of portions of three ancient regions, Kaliṅga, Utkala or Oḍra and Kosala which in course of centuries under political, social and economic pressures joined together in the twelfth century CE, and developed to form the Oriyā society as a distinct entity in the realm of India. Of all the regions, Kaliṅga was the most prominent and advanced in all respects. The original inhabitants of these regions belong to the Sabar (Savar) tribe which had a distinct civilization of its own. Thanks to the discoveries of the archaeologists, it is now conclusively proved that the pre-Āryan civilization was of a high order and it influenced the Āryan civilization in many ways. There was conflict between the two civilizations at the initial stage as is indicated in the *Ṛgveda* but in course of time, by mutual give and take, there was mutual accommodation as is indicated in the later Vedas. Even then the shades of the two civilizations remained prominently in various regions in India. The shade of Āryan civilization is distinguishable in north India whereas in the south that of pre-Āryan Dravidian civilization is distinguishable. But Orissa is a region lying between the north and the south, the synthesis has been so complete that the shades of two civilizations are not distinguishable. Thus, Orissa is the epitome of

India as its culture developed in course of centuries as a result of action and reaction of pre-Āryan and Āryan civilization.

At the initial stage when there was conflict between the two civilizations, there was a ban for the Āryans to come to Kaliṅga. While discussing the comparative sacredness of the regions inhabited by the Āryans, the non-Āryans and the mixed, Baudhāyana in his *Sūtra* mentions the regions which one should not ordinarily visit except on pilgrimage. Kaliṅga was one of those regions against which this ban was imposed.

There is no mention of any of the regions now constituted the state of Orissa in Vedic literature. But in the *Mahābhārata* there are copious references to Kaliṅga whereas Utkala, Udra or Oḍra *deśa* are occasionally mentioned.[4] In the *Mahābhārata* the inhabitants of Kaliṅga have been mentioned as Kṣatriyas and yet side by side it is mentioned that they were degraded to the rank of Śūdras as they were irreligious. There is reference in the *Mahābhārata* to the river Baitaraṇī which was in Kaliṅga and where Yudhiṣṭhira when he went out on pilgrimage performed *yajña* with the *devas*, as advised by the Sage Lomaśa. In the *Manusaṁhitā*, the Kṣatriyas of Oḍra have been denounced as degraded ones for non observance of Vedic rites.

The process of reconciliation between the Āryan and the pre-Āryan civilization started when Buddhism and Jainism, the two reformist religions became the mass religions of India. Orthodox Brahmanism received a serious jolt when the general masses turned towards the above two religions. Buddhism and Jainism spread in Orissa from the very beginning. There are copious references in Buddhist and Jaina literatures to Kaliṅga and Utkala.

The Buddhist *Jātakas* and the Jaina literature roughly covering the sixth and the seventh centuries BCE, contain descriptions of Kaliṅga and Utkala in their stories. Following are the accounts we get from the Pāli *Jātakas*.

At that time Dantapur was the capital of Kaliṅga. Once, owing to a severe drought Dantapur fell within the grip of a terrible famine. As desired by the ministers, the king of Kaliṅga deputed some Brāhmins to the king of Kuru to bring the latter's white elephant, Añjanavasabhā by name, which was believed to have possessed the power of bringing down the rains. The elephant was brought but on this occasion it failed to bring down the rains. It was thereupon decided that the prosperity of the Kurus was due to the *Kurudhamma* (*Pañchaśīlā*) observed by the king and others of that country. Therefore, the king of Kaliṅga practised the *Kurudhamma* and rain fell in his country (*Kurudhamma Jātaka*). This story of the white elephant has also been related in the *Vessantara Jātaka* in a different manner. It has been stated there that the prince Sudatta was banished along with his wife and two children by the king for having presented a white elephant to the king of Kaliṅga.

Another king of Kaliṅga was a contemporary of Aruṇa, the Assaka (Aśmaka or Aśvaka) king of Potali. Under an impulse for battle the king of Kaliṅga fought with Aruṇa without any provocation for hostilities. But he was defeated and had to give his four daughters in marriage to Aruṇa with ample riches as dowry.

In the *Sarabhaṅga Jātaka* it has been mentioned that the king of Kaliṅga along with two other kings, Aṭṭhaka and Bhīmaratta went to Sarabhaṅga to put him questions on the fate of Kandaki.

Another king of Kaliṅga, Nalikira by name, having persecuted a monk, was condemned to 'Sunakha Niraya' and *devatās* destroyed his kingdom.

We find reference to a king of Kaliṅga named Karnadu in the *Kumbhakara Jātaka.* He was a contemporary of king Nagnajita (Naggaji) of Gandhāra and king Bhīma of Vidarbha.

The following story in the '*Kaliṅga Bodhi Jātaka*' has a reference to the king of Kaliṅga.

At Dantapur the king of Kaliṅga had two sons, named Mahākaliṅga and Chullakaliṅga otherwise known as Kaliṅga Kumāra. The foretellers predicted that Chullakaliṅga would turn a monk and that his son would become the king. On this prophecy Chullakaliṅga turned so bold and obstinate that Mahākaliṅga, the moment he ascended the throne, ordered his men to imprison Chullakaliṅga who had to flee into the forest of Nimava and led the life of a recluse. Near his hermitage were living the king and queen of Maddadeśa, who had also fled from their capital, Sagala, with their daughter. In Sagala the foretellers too had predicted that the son of the princess would become the king. So all the kings of Jambudīpa wanted to marry her. Not to incur the displeasure of any of them the king fled and took shelter in the forest. It so happened that one day the princess floated a garland of mango flowers in the river. Chullakaliṅga came in for this garland and began searching for the princess. At last with due permission from the parents of the princess, he married her. The son that was born of this marriage was given the name of 'Kaliṅga'. In the meantime Mahākaliṅga died and on receiving the news Chullakaliṅga sent his son to Dantapur to one of his intimate friends. The people of Dantapur knowing the identity of the prince offered him the throne. The royal priest 'Kaliṅga Bharadvāja' began to teach him lessons on the duty of a king, etc.

According to *Dīgha Nikāya* and *Mahāvastu,* in the olden days during the reign of king Renu, Bhāratavarṣa was divided into seven political units and the name of Kaliṅga Ratha or Kaliṅga Rāṣṭra was at the top of the list. Sattabhu or Satavahu was the king of this country.[5]

According to *Mahā Govinda Sattata,* king Sattabhu was a contemporary of Dhatarattha, king of Benaras.

In *Mahāvastu,* mention has been made of another king of Dantapur whose name was Udagata.

There is no mention of the name of Kaliṅga in the list of sixteen states given in the *Aṅguttara Nikāya.* But the name of Kaliṅga appears in the list of kingdoms given in *Niddes.*

It is described in the *Mahāparinibāna Sutta* that after the death of the blessed one, a tooth of Gautama Buddha was given by a Buddhist Arhat, Khemather by name, to Brahmadatta, the king of Kaliṅga. The king raised a Stupa for the worship of this tooth and the place where the Stupa was erected came to be known as Dantapur. This fact is also corroborated by *Datha Dhātu Vaṁśam,* a Pāli work by Dhamma Kitti of Sri Lanka. According to this book the above mentioned event took place in 543 BCE.

So far we have discussed references to the kingdom of Kaliṅga only. As regards Utkala it is found that two merchants from Utkala, Tapassu and Bhāllika by name, while proceeding from the town of Pokkharavati to *Rājagraha* or (*Rājagṛha*) met the Blessed one on their way at Rajayatanamula near Uruvela. They offered food to the Buddha and listened to his sermons. In the Pāli books of *Majjhima Nikāya* and

Mahāvagga these two merchants are described as men of Bhuiyan tribe. In the *Mahāvastu* the name of Utkala has been mentioned in the list of kingdoms then existing in the Uttarapatha or northern India. In the same work, the name of Ukkala or Okkala tribe finds frequent mention in the description of different tribes of India.

In the sacred books of the Jains also there are references to Kaliṅga. It is stated in the Jain *Harivaṁśa Purāṇa* that Mahāvīra Vardhamān (599-527 BCE) preached in Kaliṅga.

Another sacred book of the Jains, informs us that the then king of Kaliṅga was a friend of the father of Mahāvīra Vardhamān and so he came to Kaliṅga to preach his religion.[6]

In the third century CE, the compositions of the *Matsya* and the *Vāyu Purāṇas* seem to have been completed. These two *purāṇas* contain the names of rivers, mountains, various regions and the names of different tribal settlements in India. It can be thus inferred from the descriptions given in these two *purāṇas* that the inhabitants of Kaliṅga were then regarded as the south Indians. The inhabitants of Oḍra *deśa* and the inhabitants of Utkala were regarded as the Vindhyans. The central Orissa was known as Tosala and the inhabitants of Tosala were not regarded as south Indians or the Vindhyans and were considered to be comparatively civilized.

Major Religious Faiths

Though the three religious beliefs, viz., Brahmanism, Buddhism and Jainism were based on different schools of philosophy they were nevertheless interrelated. Consequently, these religious beliefs were not different religions in the same sense as Hinduism and Islam. All these three religions were like the different branches of the same tree. None of them supplanted the other. They flourished side by side; sometimes one had the ascendency and sometimes another. There are evidences to show that kings following Brahmanism donated grants to the Buddhists and the Jains and also the Buddhist or the Jain rulers gave land to the Brāhmins. There was harmony and concord and no serious enmity among these religions.

In the fifth century BCE, during the rule of the Nandas, Brahmanism seems to have been the prevailing religion in Orissa for the Nanda kings followed it. What was the religion of the successors of the Nandas in Orissa is not known to us, but it can be said without any fear of contradiction that Jainism and Buddhism spread in Orissa during this period. After the conquest of Orissa by Aśoka in the third century BCE, Buddhism made rapid strides in Orissa. Aśoka's personal religion was Buddhism and the royal religion must have influenced the people. He undertook special measures for the moral uplift of the masses by appointing what may be called the ministers of morals (*Dharma Mahāmātras*).[7] From Aśokan inscription it is gathered that he particularly instructed his officers to make the wild tribes (the Atavikas) religious minded. Aśoka's *Dharma* was based on the principles of non-violence and sanctity of life and thus the foundation was laid for the spread of Buddhism among them. That the wild tribes formed the majority of the inhabitants of south Orissa of those days is known from the Pāli books and from contemporary historical records. Their descendants are still living in the Mala (not plain) areas of Ganjam and Koraput districts and in their neighbourhoods.

In the second century BCE, when Khāraveḷa ruled over Orissa, Jainism came to be the royal religion. Though he performed a *Rājasūya Yajña* according to the Vedic rites he was a staunch Jaina and took effective measures for its propagation. Again in the third century CE, Tosali appears to have become a famous centre of the Buddhists. They were Vaiṣṇavas and naturally they patronised Vaiṣṇavism in Orissa during their rule. The Mathara kings (4th-5th century CE) called themselves *Parama Daivata* which shows that they followed Brahmanism. The Vaśiṣṭhas who succeeded them were Vaiṣṇavas, for they called themselves *Parama Bhāgavatas*. The Śailodbhavas who came after the Vaśiṣṭhas were Śaivites. Towards the close of the Śailodbhava rule Śaśāṅka, the king of Karṇasuvarṇa, conquered Kaṅgoda, a kingdom carved out of Kaliṅga, and he was an enemy of Buddhism. Under him the Buddhists were badly persecuted. The atrocities committed by him on the Buddhists have been recorded by Hiuen Tsang in his accounts from which we also know that Oḍra portion of Orissa was Buddhist while in Kaliṅga and Kaṅgoda Buddhism had lost its hold.

In Harṣa, Buddhism found a strong supporter in Kaṅgoda. The Gaṅgas of Kaliṅga who ruled as contemporaries of the Śailodbhavas were Śaivites. The Karas or the Bhaumas supported Buddhism and under them Buddhism reached the height of its glory in Orissa. But there are evidences to show. That Vaiṣṇavism and Śaivism were also prevalent. Tribhuvana Mahādevī called herself Parama Vaiṣṇavī.[8] Śubhākaradeva III called himself Parameśvara. He, at the request of Vinita Tuṅga donated a village for the worship of Buddha Bhaṭṭāraka while Vinita Tuṅga himself was a Śaiva and called himself Maheśvara.

From the foregoing accounts it would be clearly known that it was a time when there was an attempt on the part of Brahmanism to absorb the declining Buddhism in its fold while Buddhism was also making efforts to retain its identity by taking in a part of Brahmanism, viz. Tantricism. From the Buddhistic ruins discovered at Udayagiri, Lalitagiri and Baudha we find traces of the influence of *tantra* cult in those days. It has to be borne in mind that this influence was not confined to Buddhism alone. Śaivism and Vaiṣṇavism also were influenced by it. In the sixth century CE, Nāgārjuna who was versed in Mayūravidyā preached his *Śūnyavāda* or the Doctrine of the Void in Orissa. In the seventh century CE, Mañjuśrī, Bodhiśrī and Chandragomi preached the Nāgāntaka school of Buddhistic philosophy in Orissa. Mayūravidyā was based on *tantra.* Nāgāntaka and Yogāntaka schools of philosophy ultimately resulted in Tantricism. When Buddhism, Śaivism and Vaiṣṇavism were all strongly influenced by Tantricism they tended to lose their separate identities.

In the eighth century CE, under the kings of the Keśari dynasty Buddhism declined and Brahmanism had ascendency. Śaṅkarāchārya, in the ninth century, came to Orissa and established the Bhogovardhana or Gobardhana Maṭha at Puri. Though the Keśaris were mainly Śaivites, Vaiṣṇavism was also spreading steadily. The twin temples at Gandharadi in Boudh are a typical specimen of the religious compromise between Śaivism and Vaiṣṇavism. These two temples are adjacent to each other and are constructed in the same style but in one of them is installed Nīlamādhava (Viṣṇu) and in the other Siddheśvara (Śiva). With the decline of the Keśaris, Śaivism also declined and there was the rise of Vaiṣṇavism. By the twelfth century, Vaiṣṇavism had occupied a position which was unassailable.

Krishnāchārya, one of the authors of *Buddha-Gāna-O-Dohā* belonged to the Vajrayāna school. Some scholars identified Vajrayāna of Buddhism with Sahajayāna of Vaiṣṇavism. There is in Bengal a sect of Vaiṣṇavas known as Sahajiā for their following the Sahajayāna doctrine. It has already been said that *Tantra* and *Yoga* had become a common feature of both Buddhism and Brahmanism before Brahmanism could absorb Buddhism in its fold. So, it is futile to speculate whether Sahajiā cult was a part of Buddhism or of Vaiṣṇavism. There is no doubt that both Brahmanism and Buddhism had contributed to give rise to the Sahajiā cult. There is greater likelihood that Sahajayāna came into being under the influence of Vaiṣṇavism on Buddhism. At the same time Tantricism had deteriorated to a very low degree. Tantricism combined with *Sahaja yāna* resulted in the grossest form of immorality and satisfaction of lust came to be regarded as a virtue. It is probable that the representation of amorous figures on the walls of temples in Orissa is due to the prevalence of the philosophy of satisfaction of lust.

Mantrayāna or Vajrayāna which prevailed in the eighth and ninth centuries was only a branch of Buddhism. It was the worth form of Tantricism. Sir Charles Eliot in his work *Hinduism and Buddhism* has shown that in Mantrayāna or Vajrayāna the worst forms of conduct in Hinduism have cleverly mixed up with Buddhism.

A branch of Vajrayāna was Vāmāchāra, which advocated the satisfaction of sexual appetite in order to attain spiritual height. Among the followers of Vajrayāna and Vāmāchāra 84 persons are known to have become famous. They are known as *Siddhas*. Some of these *Siddhas* belonged to Orissa. Krishnāchārya was famous amongst them.

In the twelfth century CE, *Nātha Dharma* began to be popular in Orissa. Balal Sen, father of Lakshman Sen, drove away the Nāthas from his territory and they came over to Orissa.

The philosophy of *Nātha Dharma* as propounded by Gorakhanātha and his Divine Master Matsyendranātha is absorbed in theory and practice, in the *Nirguṇa Bhakti* cult. Almost all the *achāryas* of the present day *Yoga* practice, follow and propagate one or some aspects of the practical Yogic methods of Gorakhanātha and his successors which they have treasured in their books, *Siddha Siddhānta Paddhati, Gorakha Paddhati, Amanaska Yoga, Gorakha Śatakam, Gorakha Siddhānta Saṅgraha, Satkarma Saṅgraha,* etc. But it is a matter of curiosity that none mentions the name of the *Nātha Siddhas* to whom they are so much indebted for their achievements, whereas historical data give ample evidence of the influence of *Nātha Dharma* since eighth century CE to the end of eighteenth century CE.

Evidence of *Nātha Dharma* in Orissa can be traced since the last quarter of the eighth century CE.. A statue of Matsyendranātha in form of Padmapāṇi Avalokiteśvara in the small forest of Rajnagar of Kendraparha subdivision is still worshipped by the Nāthas of the surrounding villages. The inscription of both the sides of the statue is in *Kuṭilalipi* or proto-*Udralipi*. The present Oriyā script was not evolved by then and the period of that script is accepted to be in between the eighth and the eleventh century CE. The prototype of the same statue is seen at Kendraparha bus stand with the same inscription and another at Trilochanpur village under Mahajanpur Grama Panchayat near Bahugram is also worshipped by the Nāthas of the surrounding villages. This proves that towards the last quarter of the ninth century, Matsyendranātha and Gorakhanātha were worshipped in Orissa as the incarnations of Viṣṇu and Śiva, respectively. The most ancient specimens of Oriyā prose and poetry are ascribed to be the works of Gorakhanātha and other Nātha Siddhas.

The theory of *Piṇḍa-Brahmāṇḍa* (cosmos in microcosm) of Gorakhanātha servers as the backbone of the Orissan Vaiṣṇava philosophy serves as the backbone of the Orissan Vaishnava philosophy of the *Pañchaśākhā* literature as in the case of the *Nirguṇa Santh Kāvyas* of the Hindi, Punjabi and Gujarati literatures of the ancient and medieval periods.

Since, the date of Sarala Das, the Nāthas of Orissa are found to be mentioned as Rudraja and Śiśuvedī Brāhmaṇa (*Śiśuvedī hoibe pañchaviṁśa sahasra brāhmaṇa*, Madhya Parva; *Śiśumuna vedena ye lakṣeka dija*, Sava Parva). They observe most of the Vedic Brahmanical rites so far as social customs are concerned with some variations. The sacred thread, according to the Nāthas, is ever pure" (*Pavitra*) even during the period of uncleanness due to birth or death. The dead body is buried seated in Yagasan in a compound specially preserved in the premises of *Maṭhas* or homestead land. The *Samādhis* are treated as sacred shrines. Śiśuveda of the Nāthas is regarded as the fifth Veda. A person from any caste or religious sect can accept *Nātha Dharma*, but he must use the title of 'Nātha' after his name after due initiation. Hundreds of *Maṭhas*, *Pīṭhas* and *Gadis* of the Nātha cult are scattered all over Orissa. Although idolatry is forbidden in *Nātha Dharma*, it got mixed up first with Buddhism, then with Hinduism. Buddhist and Brahman idols were accepted by the Nāthas. It is the *Nātha Dharma* which made *Yoga* popular in Orissa.

One interesting fact is that Orissa is the state where in ancient times *Atharvaveda* was the procreating Veda. This was known when research was made on *Paipallāda Sūtra* of *Atharvaveda* which was taken to be lost, but manuscripts of which were found in many villages in Orissa. When *Atharvaveda* was downgraded during the ascendency of Brahmanism many changed over to *Yajur Veda*, but they could not dispense with some rituals of *Atharvaveda* during ceremonies such as marriage, etc.

That the influence of these religious currents and cross-currents worked in Orissa cannot be gainsaid.

Under Chodogaṅgadeva (twelfth century), Vaiṣṇavism was firmly rooted in Orissa. It is said that Chodagaṅgadeva was the creator of the Vaiṣṇava era in Orissa.[9] Rāmānuja came to Puri sometime between 1122 and 1137 CE, and gave a strong impetus to Vaiṣṇavism. The temple of Alarnāthā at Brahmagiri in Puri district was constructed about this time. The image of Viṣṇu along with those of Lakṣmī, Rukmiṇī and Sarasvatī is worshipped there. Rāmānuja tried to bring about certain changes in the worship of Jagannātha, but there was strong opposition. Although Jagannātha came to be regarded as an incarnation of Viṣṇu, a separate temple was constructed in the compound of the temple of Jagannātha at Puri to install Lakṣmī, the consort of Viṣṇu.

In the twelfth century also Jayadeva came to Puri and preached the cult of love of Rādhā and Kṛṣṇa, but it took long three hundred years till the coming of Shri Chaitanya for this cult to be firmly rooted in the Orissan soil.

Curiously enough there was no trace of Rādhā-Kṛṣṇa worship either in Orissa or in Bengal during that period. In the list of ten *avatāras*, Jayadeva has not included Kṛṣṇa, although His amorous life is depicted in his entire work.

The thirteenth century CE, witnessed the activities of Narasiṁha Muni Narahari *tīrtha* and Jagannātha *tīrtha* who preached Vaiṣṇavism in Orissa. In the 14th century Narasiṁha Bhārati and Rāghava preached Vaiṣṇavism of Mādhavāchārya school. During the rule of Gaṅga kings particularly from Anaṅgavimadeva III religious teachers of Mādhavāchārya school preached Vaiṣṇavism under royal patronage. Mādhavāchārya in his late years became a devotee of Madanagopāla or Gopālakṛṣṇa. At his instance some of his disciples built temples dedicated to Gopālakṛṣṇa. From that time onwards worship of Gopālakṛṣṇa received royal patronage.

The temple of the Sun God at Konark was built in the thirteenth century CE, Sun worship had been in vogue even from the Vedic Age. In course of time the Sun was identified with Viṣṇu. With this identification certain ceremonials connected with the Sun worship was transferred to the worship of Kṛṣṇa-Vāsudeva. Trivikrama (the dwarf incarnation of Viṣṇu) is also another name for the Sun. It has to be remembered that the worship of Viṣṇu is almost as old as the Sun worship. It is difficult to say with any certainty when Sun worship was introduced in Orissa, but from the existence of an image of the Sun on a chariot drawn by four horses in the Ananta cave of Khandagiri which was carved in the second century BCE, some scholars are inclined to believe that Sun worship was a part of Viṣṇu worship even in the second century BCE. But such a conclusion from an isolated representation is hazardous and cannot be relied upon.

It is quite probable that during the Keśari kings Sun worship was introduced in Orissa. There is a representation of the Sun God drawn by four horses on one of the walls in the compound of the Liṅgarāja temple at Bhubaneswar. There are traces of Sun worship at Jajpur. There were pillars with Garuḍa seated on them but they were damaged or destroyed by the Muslim conquerors. On the steps leading from the Varāhanātha temple to the banks of the Baitaraṇī there is a representation of the Sun God drawn by seven horses. Sun worship reached its zenith in Orissa when Narasiṁhadeva I constructed the Sun temple at Konark which is known as the Black Pagoda in the western world.

There was a time when the Sun God at Konark elicited great reverence like Jagannātha at Puri. Though the Sun worship had been known from the Vedic time it was with the immigration of the Magas of Persia that Sun worship found popular favour in India. The Magas were Sun worshippers. Besides the Magas of Persia, another race also called the Magas Śakadvīpa confirmed the Sun worship in India. Of the latter Magas there is a tradition that Samba, the son of Kṛṣṇa, was cursed by his father to be inflicted with leprosy whereupon he worshipped Maitreya, i.e. the Sun to recover from the disease. The Sun God advised him to invite some Maga Brāhmaṇas of Śakadvīpa for his worship. Among the Maga Brāhmaṇas there was a sect called the 'Koṇas' and another sect called the 'Arkas'. The name of Konark originated probably from the names of these two sects of Brāhmins.[10] With the spread of Vaiṣṇavism from the eighth century CE, onwards incarnations like Kūrma (Tortoise), Varāha (Boar), Nṛsiṁha (Man-lion), etc., came to be worshipped.

There is a tradition that Narasiṁhadeva I built a temple at Remuna and it was dedicated to Madangopāla.

Jagannātha has been described as Viṣṇu in a copper plate grant of Narasiṁhadeva IV. In the same copper plate it is mentioned that Gaṅgeśvaradeva had constructed the temple of Jagannātha. Narasiṁhadeva flourished in the fourteenth century CE. By that time in other parts of India Gopālakṛṣṇa had totally eclipsed. Kṛṣṇa-Vāsudeva and the cult of love of Rādhā and Kṛṣṇa had obtained a firm footing. But this cult seems to have been completely unknown to Orissa till the middle of the fifteenth century CE.[11]

Puruṣottamadeva who succeeded Kapilendradeva is known to have made grants of land to one Posteśvarabhaṭṭa in which he solicited the blessings of Madangopāla installed at Remuna. It was Puruṣottamadeva who is said to have brought the image of Śakhigopāla from Kāñchī and installed it in his palace. But till the reign of Puruṣottamadeva there was no worship of Rādhā along with Kṛṣṇa.

Shri Chaitanya came to Orissa in 1509 CE, and stayed there for 15 years during the reign of Pratāpaṛudradeva who succeeded Puruṣottamadeva. Among the aristocrats, particularly among the courtiers of Orissa, the works of Vidyāpati and Chaṇḍīdāsa had been very popular. Ramananda Rai, the Governor of Deccan territory of Orissa, was imbued with the spirit of the new cult of love and his exposition of the philosophy of love before Shri Chaitanya has been described in details in the Chaitanya Charitāmṛta. He was so absorbed in religious matters that he ultimately resigned his post to devote himself entirely to religion based on the philosophy of love. It is said that he had memorized all the works of Vidyāpati and Chaṇḍīdāsa. Thus, the field had been prepared for the propagation of the cult of love and with the advent of Shri Chaitanya the cult of love easily found favour with the people.

Contemporary literature of the period shows that Shri Chaitanya's cult of love captivated the minds of the people of the upper classes only, but the common people still thought that Jagannātha was the be-all and end-all in religious life.

There would have been a struggle but as Shri Chaitanya accepted Jagannātha as his Lord, Vaiṣṇavism as propounded by him was accepted by the masses.

This is briefly the history of development of various cults and religious faiths in Orissa overlapping one another in the course of about a thousand years. But curiously enough all these faiths have been epitomised to Jagannātha who throughout the ages has been the centre of religious life in Orissa.

The religious life of Orissa is inextricably bound up with Jagannātha at Puri. For the people of Orissa Jagannātha is the manifestation of the Supreme Being. There have been, from time to time, revolutionary changes in the popular religion of the country. Buddhism, Jainism, Śaivism, Vaiṣṇavism and Tantricism all have exercised a strong influence on the religious beliefs of the people. Sometimes royal patronage has lent support to one particular cult or another, but the glory of Jagannātha continues undiminished as ever. The history of the religion of the Oriyā people is, so to speak, the history of Jagannātha who has absorbed in himself all faiths in some form or other.

In the nineteenth century, a religion known as *Mahimā Dharma* became popular in some parts of Orissa. Its philosophy is not yet clearly defined. It enforces strict observance of rules relating caste system and Brahmanism. It is not Buddhism, nor Jainism. It is a religion on its own merit.

Another reformist movement named *Brahmo Samāja* made its appearance in Orissa in the second half of the nineteenth century. The *Samāja* wanted to purify the habitual Hinduism in which a number of superstitions, beliefs had come in and established a society free from caste system and prejudices against woman and idolatry in all form. But it strictly adhered to the philosophy of the ancient Vedic period.

Islam came to Orissa along with the Afghan invasion in the last half of the sixteenth century, but in spite of its existence for about last 400 years it could not make much headway in Orissa. Because the strength of the Bhakti cult of Vaiṣṇavism prevented conversion of Hindus into Islam.

Towards the end of the nineteenth century Christianity came to Orissa. A number of Churches were established in various parts of the state, particularly in the tribal areas. The effect of Christianity on the society as a whole has not been significant. Even those tribal people who have been converted into Christianity go their own way in spite of the new religion which they have adopted.

From the above account it will be seen that really the culture of Orissa has been one of synthesis of various faiths and cultures. Syncretic Jagannātha has been the centre of this synthesis all along. The cultural synthesis of Orissa is not to be found in any other state of India in the same degree as in Orissa.

References

1. Devendra Kumar Rajaram Patil, *Cultural History from Vāyu Purāṇa,* Motilal Banarsidass, Delhi, 1946, p. 46.
2. Subodh Kapoor (ed.), *The Indian Encyclopaedia,* vol. I, Genesis Publishing Pvt. Ltd., Delhi, 2012, p. 7311.
3. Amalananda Ghosh, *An Encyclopaedia of Indian Archaeology,* BRILL, Leiden, 1990, p. 24.
4. N.C. Behuria (ed.), *Orissa State Gazetteer, Orissa State,* vol. II, Bhubaneswar, 1991, p. 2.
5. *Ibid.*, p. 4.
6. K.C. Panigrahi, *History of Orissa,* Kitab Mahal, Cuttack, 1981, p. 296.
7. Harihar Panda, *History of Orissa,* "Kaliṅga Under the Maurya Rule", Kitab Mahal, Cuttack, 1997, p. 32.
8. *Ibid.*, p. 75.
9. Yajna Kumar Sahu, *Odisha Itihasa,* Part I, Ganga Samrajya, Nalanda, Cuttack, 1991, p. 195.
10. N.C. Behuria, *op. cit.*, p. 11.
11. *Ibid.*

Chapter II

Indian Temples

The Concepts

Temples are not mere symbols of our religion but representatives of our culture, engineering skills and traditions. Generally speaking a temple is a "Place of Worship". It is also called the "House of God". To add more, the Hindu temple is the enshrined deity's house (*devālaya*), and his or her palace (*prāsāda*), where the priests cater to his or her daily needs. It is a holy site (*tīrtha*) where the devotees come to perform the circumambulation (*Pradakṣiṇā*) to earn the religious merit and spiritual attainment. Stella Kramrisch has defined temple as *Monument of Manifestation* in her book *The Hindu Temple.* He has also mentioned that the super structure of the temple is the manifestation of God.[1] The temple is one of the prominent and enduring symbols of Indian culture: it is the most graphic expression of religious fervour, metaphysical values and aesthetic aspiration. The idea of temple originated centuries ago in the universal ancient conception of God in a human form, which required a habitation, a shelter and this requirement resulted in a structural shrine. India's temple architecture is developed from the Sthapati's and Silpi's creativity. A small Hindu temple consists of an inner sanctum, the *garbhagṛha* or womb chamber; a small square room with completely plain walls having a single narrow doorway in the front, inside which the image is housed and other chambers which are varied from region to region according to the needs of the rituals.

Every element of the temple, its structure, sculpture, design and motifs are all imbued with intrinsic meaning. The statue enshrined is the manifestation of the deity from which divine energy radiates in different directions from the *garbhagṛha.* From top to bottom the Hindu temple seeks to represent everything of which the cosmic world *Brahmāṇḍa,* the entire universe, is composed of: the earthly world, the heavenly world, *Pṛthvī, Ākāśa* with *Svarga,* and *Pātāla,* respectively.[2] That is why on the walls of a Hindu temple one can see the representations of men, women, children, animals, seas, mountains, houses, forts, places, villages, huts, etc. copulation amongst men and among animals since it is through this mode of life that creation takes place. The Hindu temple architecture, i.e. its morphology, follows the requirements of man's vision of the cosmos which he wants to recreate on the earth; it is not the fancy of the architect. Visions differ, therefore forms differ, but forms are not experiments of architects.

The temple also contains the images of gods and goddesses as well as semi-divine and mythical beings, including half-human and half-animal or half-bird and half-reptile forms, as described in Hindu mythologies contained in epics, *Purāṇas,* and *Kāvyas.* The world of waters with fish, tortoise, crocodile, coral, plants, rocks, etc. which constitute the life below the seas is also represented. Underlying all these so simple yet so complex ideas is the water cosmology (science of universe) as well as water cosmogony (origin of the universe) which means that water is the basis of all creation and sustainer. It is for this very reason that from the Gupta time itself the temple pillars are shown emerging from *kalaśa* or water-pot, and the finial or top is embellished with a *kalaśa.*

Hindu and Non-Hindu Views on Sacred Structure

Thus, a Hindu views his temple slightly differently that a Christian views his church or a Muslim views his mosque. For a Christian, the church is just a "place of worship", it is neither the House of God nor Mini Cosmos; for a Muslim, the mosque is just a "place for offering prayer to God". A Hindu may worship many gods at one and the same time since he believes that in whatever form or forms one may worship, all will eventually reach God, the only one the ultimate Reality "as wherever the rain water from heaven may fall it goes to the ocean", similarly "prayers offered to one and all gods go to God alone".[3]

The Placements of Images

The sculptures representing gods and goddesses can be placed anywhere and worshipped even under a tree, or over a platform, or in a cave, or under a rock-shelter, or one the bank of river, or a tank, or ocean; in fact, anywhere and everywhere, However, from purely temporal point of view, a temple is a cover to protect the image from the vagaries of nature as well as animals. A temple may be either in the form of a huge sculptured rock, called rock-cut temple, or else it is a built-structure using bricks, or wood, or stone pieces; sometimes even terracotta is used.

Merits Gained by Temple Building

In the *Śiva Purāṇa* (5.51.113-22), we are told of the merit gained by a person who builds a temple to the goddess, whether built of stone, wood, or mud, the passage reading:

He who builds a temple to the goddess attains the benefit which a person who worships everyday through *Yoga* attains in plenty. That virtuous soul who builds the temple for the glorious mother enables a thousand past and a thousand future members of his family to attain liberation.

The sins committed by a person in a crore of births, whether they be small or big, are quelled at the very moment when the foundation for the temple of the glorious mother is laid.

The glorious great Ambā.... is the most important among all the deities. He who causes her temple to be built attains established power in every birth.....

He is honoured in the Maṇidvīpa for as many thousand years as the number of years the brickwork holds good.[4]

Types of Temples

Though the Indian temples are classified under two broad groups under the names Temples of North India and Temples of South India yet the Indian *Śilpāchāryas* and ancient architects have classified the Indian temples under the following twenty heads. They are enumerated thus[5].

1.	Meru	2.	Mandara
3.	Kaliāsa	4.	Vimāna-figure
5.	Nandana	6.	Samudga
7.	Padma	8.	Garuḍa
9.	Nandin	10.	Vardhana
11.	Kunjara	12.	Guharāja
13.	Vṛṣa	14.	Haṁsa
15.	Sarvatobhadra	16.	Ghaṭa
17.	Siṁha	18.	Rotunda
19.	Quadrangle	20.	Octangle

All these different kinds of temples have been described by Varāhamihira in his *Bṛhatsaṁhitā.* He Says:

"the Meru is sexangular, has twelve storeys, variegated windows, and four entrances. It is 32 cubits wide."

"the Mandāra is 30 cubits in extent, has ten storeys and turrets"

The Kailāsa, too, has turrets, and eight storeys; it measures 28 cubits.

The Vimāna is 21 cubits in extent, and has latticed windows.

The Nandana has six stories and sixteen cupolas; it measures 32 cubits.

The Samudga (i.e. round box)is round.

The Padma (i.e. lotus) has the shape of lotus, measure eight cubits, has one spire and only storey.

The Garuḍa and Nandin show the form of the sun-eagle, are 24 cubits wide, must be constructed with seven storeys, and adorned with twenty cupolas.

The Kunjara (i.e. elephant) has a figure like an elephant's back and is sixteen cubits long, and brord at, the bottom.

The Guharāja likewise measures sixteen cubits. Both have a roof with three dormer windows.

The Vṛṣa (i.e bull) has a single storey and one turret, is everywhere round, and measures twelve cubits.

The Haṁsa has the form of a swan.

The Ghaṭa, being shaped like a water-jar, has an extension of eight cubits.

The Sarvatobhadra has four entrances, many summits, many beautiful dormer windows and five storeys, its extent being twenty-five cubits.

The Siṁha is a building with twelve angles, and is covered by lions; it is eight cubit wide.

The four remaining (namely, Rotunda, Quadrangle, octangle and sixteen-angle) are dark (in the interior). The quadrangle has five cupolas (whereas the rest have one only)".[6]

Unfortunately, we donot find instances of all these kinds of temples in existence in India. The existing temples in India may be grouped under four classes, namely–

(a) The Orissa type, specially found in Orissa.

(b) The Bengali type in Bengal.

(c) The Gujarati type in Gujarat.

(d) The Dravidian or south Indian type.

According to the *Śukranīti,* however, there are only sixteen kinds of temples. It says:

> "(the temples are) to be of the Meru or some other of the sixteen types; to be beautiful, round, square or of some other mechanical form; to have *Maṇḍapas* or halls, walls, *Gopuras* or central gates; to have height twice or thrice the width, to have good images inside made according to the prescribed rules, to have water at the foot and to be well painted or decorated".[7]

We give below the names of these sixteen kinds of temples with their characteristics[8]:

Type	*Domes*	*Stones*	*Height (in cubit)*	*Width (in cubit)*	
1.	Meru	1,000	125	1,000	1,000
2.	Mandāra	875	110	375	875
3.	Rkṣamak	766	56	766	766
4.	Dyumani	670	84	670	670
5.	Chandraśekhara	586	74	586	586
6.	Malyavān	513	65	513	513
7.	Pārijāta	449	57	449	449
8.	Ratnagasa	393	50	393	393
9.	Dhatuman	344	44	344	344
10.	Padmakośa	301	36	301	301
11.	Puṣpahasa	263	32	263	263
12.	Sikara	230	28	230	230
13.	Svastika	210	25	201	201
14.	Mahāpadma	176	22	176	176
15.	Padmakūṭa	154	19	154	154
16.	Vijaya	135	17	135	135

If we compare this list of temples as given by the sage Śukra and the one in *Bṛhatsaṁhitā*, we find only *Meru, Mandāra* and *Padma* (*Mahāpadma*) in common.

The *Śukranīti* describes the *Meru* temple thus: "A *Meru* temple is that which has one thousand domes, has one hundred and twenty-five storeys, is one thousand cubits wide and one thousand cubits high".

The temple should have a *maṇḍapa* or a hall which is to be adapted to each and one fourth less than the temple in height.

There is an *Oriyā Śilpa* manuscript called *Bhuvanapraveśa*[9], which gives the names of several temples with their sketches. It belongs to Sri Babaji Maharana, son of Govinda Maharana of Puri. The reading of this manuscript unfortunately is so corrupt that it is next impossible to restore the original version. So, we are unable to restore all the names given in that Ms. We can make out only the following names:

1. Mahāmmeru
2. Mandāra
3. Kailāsa
4. Bhadra
5. Keśari
6. Sri Vatsa
7. Nandī
8. Vṛṣa
9. Haṁsa
10. Garuḍa
11. Laghu Vimāna

In various *Śilpa śāstras* we find detailed instructions for the construction of all types of buildings and also rules of proportion for the sculpting of different categories of images. It is from these *Śilpa śāstras* that we come to know about the types of temples. Regional variations led to Hindu temples being broadly classified into the northern type (*Nāgara*), belonging to the area between Himālāyas and the Vindhyas and the southern type (*Draviḍa*), falling in the region between river Kṛṣṇā to Kanyākumārī. A third one, taking the features of both these types is the *Vesara*, located between the Vindhyas and the Kṛṣṇā. Thus in broad sense the Indian *Śilpa śāstras* recognize three main styles of temple architecture known as the *Nāgara*, the *Draviḍa* and the Vesara.[10] However, the distinction rests on the shape of the tower, the ground plan and the elevation.

Nāgara Temple Style

Nāgara types of temples are the typical northern Indian temples with curvilinear *śikhara* spire topped by *amlakaśilā.*[11] This style was developed during fifth century CE. The Nāgara style is characterized by a beehive-shaped and multi-layered tower, called *śikhara.* The layers of this tower are topped by a large round cushion like element called *āmlaka.* The plan is based on a square but the walls are sometimes so segmented, that the tower appears circular in shape. Advancement in the architecture is found in temples belonging to later periods, in which the central shaft is surrounded by many smaller reproductions of itself, creating a visual effect of a fountain.

Draviḍa Temple Style

Dravidian architecture is a style of architecture that emerged thousands of years ago in the Indian subcontinent. They consist primarily of pyramid shaped temples with cupola-formed *śikharas.* These temples are dependent on intricate carved stone in order to create a step design consisting of many statues of deities, warriors, kings and dancers. The majority of the existing buildings are located in the south Indian states. The earliest monuments of this school can be seen at Mamallapuram and at Kanchipuram.

Vesara Temple Style

Vesara type of temples contains elements of both *Nāgara* and *Draviḍa* styles. This style is also described in some texts as the 'Central Indian Temple Architecture Style' or 'Deccan Architecture'. The trend was started by the Chālukyas of Bādāmi (500-753 CE) who built temples in a style is that was essentially a mixture of the *Nāgara* and the *Draviḍa* styles, further refined by the Rāṣṭrakūṭas of Manyakheta (750-983 CE) in Ellora, Chālukyas of Kalyāṇī (983-1195 CE) in Lakkundi, Dambal, Gadag, etc. and epitomized by the Hoysālas (1000-1330 CE). This style mostly prevalent in the Deccan. The ground plan of the temples of this style is starshaped or polygonal. The temple consists of shrine, anti-chamber and hall with aisles and porch.

References

1. Stella Kramrisch, *The Hindu Temple,* vol. I, Motilal Banarsidass, Delhi, 1976, p. 7.
2. S.P. Gupta, *Elements of Indian Art,* D.K. Printworld, Delhi, 2009, p. 31.
3. *Ibid.*, pp. 31-32.

4. *Śiva Purāṇa,* tr. "A board of Scholars", AITMS vols. 1-4, 1983 reprint, IV, p. 1668.
5. P.N. Bose, *Principles of Indian Silpasastra,* Bharatiya Publishing House, Delhi, 1978, p. 71.
6. *J.R.A.S.* (N.S), VI, pp. 317-321.
7. B.K. Sarkar, *Śukranīti,* ch. IV, sec. IV, pp.166-167.
8. *Ibid.,* p.167.
9. P.N. Bose, *op. cit.,* p. 74.
10. P. Acharya, *Studies in Orissan History, Archaeology and Archives,* Cuttack Student's Store, Cuttack, 1969, p. 386.
11. M.A. Dhaky, *The Indian Temple Forms,* Delhi, 1977, p. 7.

Chapter III

Orissan Temples

Orissa is famous for her historic antiquities and religious monuments. Numerous temples representing the various branches of Kaliṅga School of Architecture are found in Orissa enchanting the tourists, historians, archaeologists and architects from all over India and abroad. The temple building activities in Orissa can be seen in the series of beautiful temples dating from sixth century CE to sixteenth century CE. The concentration of the largest number of temples all over the state has made it a centre of unique attraction for the scholars, visitors, indologists and others since the evolution of the temples. It may be noted that out of the five different types of architecture such as devotional, memorial, civil, military and domestic we mainly come across the devotional type of architecture in Orissa while others have disappeared with the ravages of time and power.[1]

General Features

The concept of temples originated centuries past with the idea of God in a human form. Such a form warranted a habitation, a shelter and this need resulted in structural edifices. In very early period such a shrine might have been made of wood, thatch and bamboo, but it soon became a sanctum of stone. The stone sanctum was known as the *garbhagṛha* literally womb house, and it was a small room often square, with completely plain walls and a single narrow doorway in front. The outer walls of the sanctum were often decorated with figural sculptures relating to the god within. Except in very rare cases these shrines often face the east so that they are lit by the rays of the rising sun. With the growth of temple building activity various texts came into being fixing norms for different categories of architectural devices. In Orissa we have evidence of a number of specialized texts which emphasized the importance of various features that never became prominent in other parts of the entire sub continent. In Orissan temple architecture each temple type and each individual member thereof, however, small, has been given a distinctive name and the measurements of the components, invariably operating under the precise laws of proportions laid down, though in cryptic terms. Further the canonical tradition is transmitted from father to son among a few surviving families of architects.

The builders of the Orissan temples gave vent to their feelings on the basis of indigenous canonical texts like *Bhubana pradīpa, Śilpa Pothī, Śilpa śāstra, Vāstu śāstra Upaniṣad, Śilparatnākara, Śilpasāriṇī, Śilpa Prakāśa, Padma Keśara, Deula Mapāguṇagara, Bhubana Prabeśa, Soudhikāgama,* etc. indicating the standard achieved by our ancestors in the field of temple architecture. To add more, *Bhubana pradīpa*[2] a treatise on temple architecture describes three types of temples, the *rekhā, bhadra* and the *khākharā.* Much emphasis is placed in this text on the exact proportions and height of different parts of the walls. The text details 36 types of *rekhā* temples, five varieties of *bhadra* temples and three types of *khākharā* temples with derailed measurements of each type.[3] The temples of Orissa resolve them-selves into three broad architectural orders: the *rekhā, pīḍha* (*bhadra*) and *khākharā.* In a typical Orissan temple of nature plan the first two order, *rekhā* and *pīḍha* go side by side and form two component parts of one architectural scheme. The *rekhā* order becomes the standard plan for the *vimāna* which houses the image or symbol of the presiding deity while the *pīḍha* order becomes the standard plan for the *mukhaśālā.* The earliest *mukhaśālās* are however, rectangular in shape and have sloping terraced roof, flat on top, supported by pillars. In the process of evolution the pillars disappeared, rectangular plan was abandoned in favour of a square plan and the flat terraced roof developed into pyramidal roof. While the *rekhā* and *pīḍha* orders are employed for temples of all religious sects, including the Śākta, the *khākharā* order is employed for temples dedicated only to Śakti worship.

The interior plan of the temples of both the *rekhā* and *pīḍha* order are square though externally they are broken by offset projections. The temples of *rekhā* and *pīḍha* order can be divided into four principal parts along the vertical plane, namely, the *piṣṭa* (platform or the pedestal), *bāḍa* (perpendicular wall), the *gaṇḍi* (body, curvilinear spire or *śikhara* in case of *rekhā* temple and pyramidal roof in case of *pīḍha* temple) and *mastaka* (head or crowning element). Of these the *piṣṭa* do not form an essential part of the temple proper for there are examples in which the *piṣṭa* is absent.

The main components of the *bāḍa* are the *pābhāga* (base mouldings), *jāṅgha* (vertical portion of the wall) and *baraṇḍa* (set of mouldings demarcating the *bāḍa* from the *gaṇḍi*). The *bāḍas* of the early temples are, thus *tryaṅga* (three divisioned), but with the increasing height of the temples at a late stage, they developed into *pañchaṅga* (five divisioned), the *jāṅgha* being subdivided into upper and lower storey by one or a set of mouldings know as *bandhana* or *Madhya bandhana*. The surface of the *bāḍa* is further demarcated by projections or *pagas* (*rathas*) which run vertically up the structure. In the earlier examples there is only one projection in the middle dividing the wall into three *rathakas* or *pagas*. The central projection called the *rāhā* runs continuously up the height of the temple where as the flanking subsidiary *pagas* terminate beneath the *baraṇḍa*. In the course of evolution the general trend to towards. In the course of evolution the general trend is towards elaboration and this *tri-ratha* plan evolves into *pañcharatha*. The corner *paga* is called *kaṇikā* whereas the intermediary *paga* is called *anuratha*. The recesses in between the *pagas* are called *anuratha* recesses. With still increase of projections in the later temples the plan becomes *sapta-ratha* and *nava-ratha*. In *sapta-ratha* temples one projection called *anuraha*[4] appears between the *rāhā* and *anuaratha* and in the *nava-ratha* temple in addition to *anuraha* one more projection is added in between the *anuratha* and *kaṇikā* known as *pari-ratha*.[5] This elaboration also takes place in the *pābhāga*, where the number of mouldings is increased from three to five and in the *baraṇḍa* where the number of mouldings is greatly increased, in some cases to ten.[6] The *bāḍa* of the *mukhaśālā* is similarly decorated though the centre projection in it becomes more pronounced and completely dominates the decorative programme.

Up to the *baraṇḍa* there is hardly any distinction between the *rekhā* and *pīḍha* temples. But it is the *gaṇḍi* that these two orders assume their individual peculiarities. The silhouette of the *śikhara* in the *rekhā* temple inclines inwards in a gradual convex curve, this being more pronounced towards the top in later temples. The *śikhara* is divided into several *pagas*. The early temples with *tri-ratha bāḍa* have *pañcha ratha* plan for the *śikhara*. The *rāhā* is a vertical extension of the *rāhā-paga* of the *bāḍa*, but *kaṇikā* and *anuratha* begin above the *baraṇḍa* and are completely independent in alignment from the subsidiary *pagas* of the *bāḍa*. It is not until the development of a full fledged *pañcha ratha* design for the *bāḍa* in the tenth century CE that the *pagas* of the *bāḍa* and *śikhara* are harmoniously aligned. The *kaṇikā paga* is subdivided into a number of *bhūmis* (planes or tiers) each of which is composed of a number of mouldings (*bhūmi-baraṇḍis*) surmounted by a miniature *āmalā* called *bhūmi-āmalā*. The *anuratha* in some examples consists of horizontal mouldings superimposed one above the other continuously up to the *bisama*. The *rāhā* is divided in to horizontal divisions like the *anuratha*. The cross section at any point of the *śikhara* is square.[7]

The *mastaka* of the *rekhā* temple consists of *beki* (recessed cylindrical portion above the *bisma*), *āmalaka* (ribbed disk), *khapūri* (skull; a flat bell-shaped member) and *kalaśa* on which is placed the *āyudha* of the presiding deity. The cross section of the *mastaka* is circular.

The *gaṇḍi* or roof of the *pīḍha* temple consists of a number of *pīḍhas* diminishing in a pyramidal shape till the topmost *pīḍha* is reduced to about a half of the lowest one. The *pīḍhas* in later temples are usually grouped into tiers called *potalas*, separated from one another by recessed vertical walls called *kanthi*.

The *khākharā* temple is invariably oblong in plan. The *gaṇḍi* is composed other like that of a *rekhā* as in the Vaitāl temple in Bhubaneswar or like that of a *pīḍha* with certain minor differences as in the Gaurī temple in Bhubaneswar. The cross section all through is however, rectangular. The *mastaka* is distinguished by barrel-vaulted elongated roof called *khākharā*. The shape of the roof as Debala Mitra has suggested is a modified survival of the primitive hunts with a semi-cylindrical roof resting on a framework of timber or split bamboos and having a hemispherical end on either side.[8]

The hollow interior above *garbhagṛha* in a *rekhā* temple is in the shape of a pyramid tapering upwards to form a solid block at the top. To ensure the stability of the structure a ceiling called *garbhamuda* is placed above the *garbhagṛha*. In larger temples the process is repeated so that there is a second ceiling known as *ratnamuda* closing the hollow chamber above the *garbhamuda*.[9] The interior of the *pīḍha* temple is plain and covered by a corbelled ceiling. In a few cases the ceilings are decorated. In early temples corbelled arches are cut above the lintel of the *vimāna* doorway. In later temples they appear even above the door ways and windows of the *mukhaśālā*. In addition to the *vimāna* and the *mukhaśālā* two more structure known as *naṭa mandira* (festival hall) and *bhōgamaṇḍapa* (hall of offerings) were introduced on the same axis during the Gaṅga period.

Sculpture

One of the distinctive feature of the Orissan temple as has been rightly observed by Dehejia is the completely plain treatment of the interior with all the carving being reserved for the exterior wall.[10] The exterior wall is marked by overall clarity of the total design in plan and elevation. Each individual architectural unity is clearly defined as a self containing element, each image is well contained within its pillar boundaries, adhering closely to the surface, "each panel to its place, each image to its ground".[11]

The *pagas* are generally designed as miniature shrines (*muṇḍīs*) complete with niche. There are four basic types of *muṇḍīs* carved on the walls, three of which are replicas of the major architectural orders: the *rekhā*, *pīḍha* and *khākharā*. The fourth type which is very popular on the earliest temples is the *vajra-muṇḍī* whose crowning elements consist of a miniature *vajra-mastaka* of two superimposed Chaitya medallions. On the early temples the subsidiary *pagas* of the *bāḍa* are designed as *vajra-muṇḍīs*. Smaller *vajra-muṇḍī* appear on the *anuratha* recesses of the *śikhara*. With the development of the two storey *jāṅgha*, *khākharā-muṇḍī* and *pīḍha-muṇḍī* become standard design respectively for the lower *jāṅgha* and upper *jāṅgha*. In the eleventh century miniature *śikharas* or *aṅga-śikharas* were introduced as a decorative feature on the *śikhara*. They are seen aligned in a horizontal row at the base of the *śikhara* or superimposed one above the other in diminishing size on the *anuratha pagas.*

The *rāhā* niche house a *pārśva-devatā,* a deity connected with the presiding deity of the temple. In a Śiva temple the niches display the images of Pārvatī or Mahiṣāsuramardinī, Gaṇeśa and Kārttikeya. On Vaiṣṇava shrines the *pārśva-devatās* are usually Varāha, Nṛsiṁha, and Trivikrama, three of the ten *avatāras* of Viṣṇu

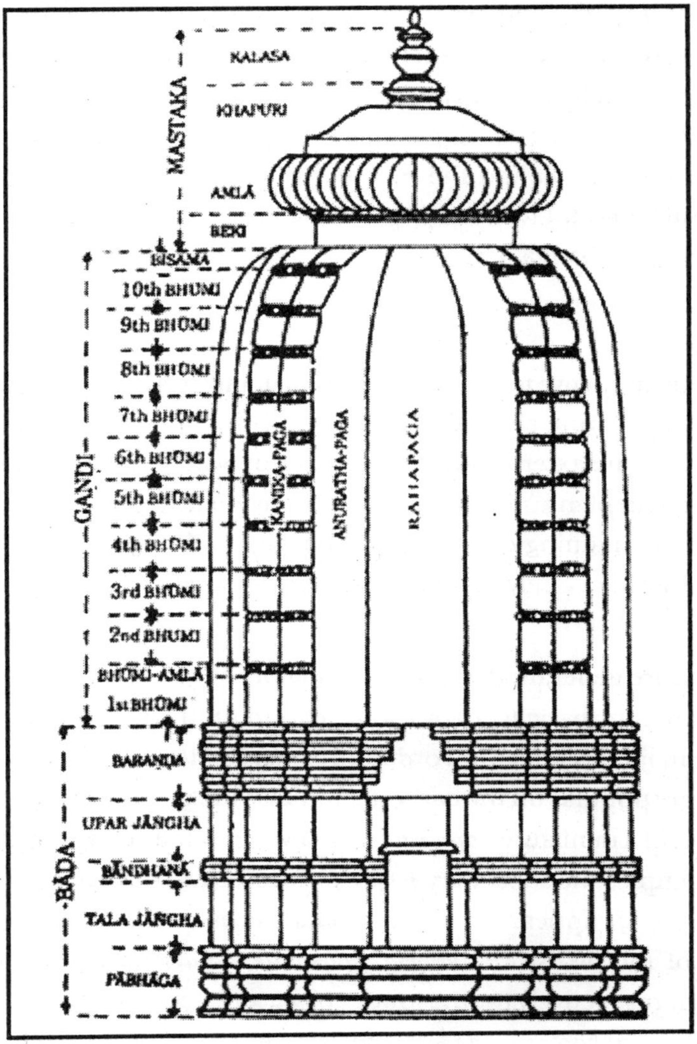

Fig. 1. Elevation of *rekhā deula*

while in the Śākta temples there are generally housed three different forms of the enshrined deity. The niches of the subsidiary *pagas* in early temples generally house images of various aspects of Śiva or other Brahmanical deities while in Śākta shrines these niches are filled with *kanyās* and loving couples.

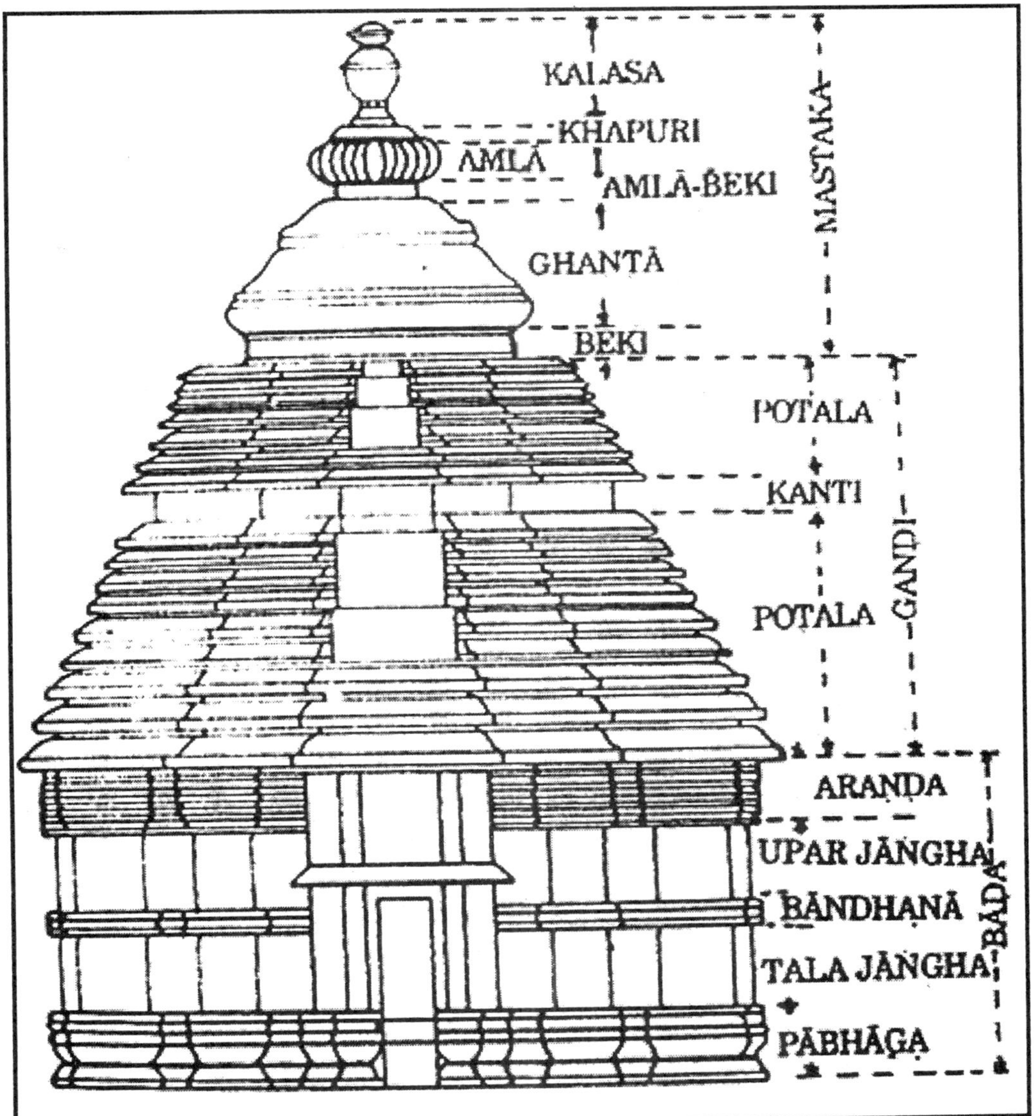

Fig. 2. Elevation of *pīḍhā deula*

The introduced in the eleventh century appear on their respective positions on the lower *jāṅgha* of the *kaṇikā pagas*, while their *śaktis* making appearance in the twelfth century occupy the upper *kaṇikā* niches.

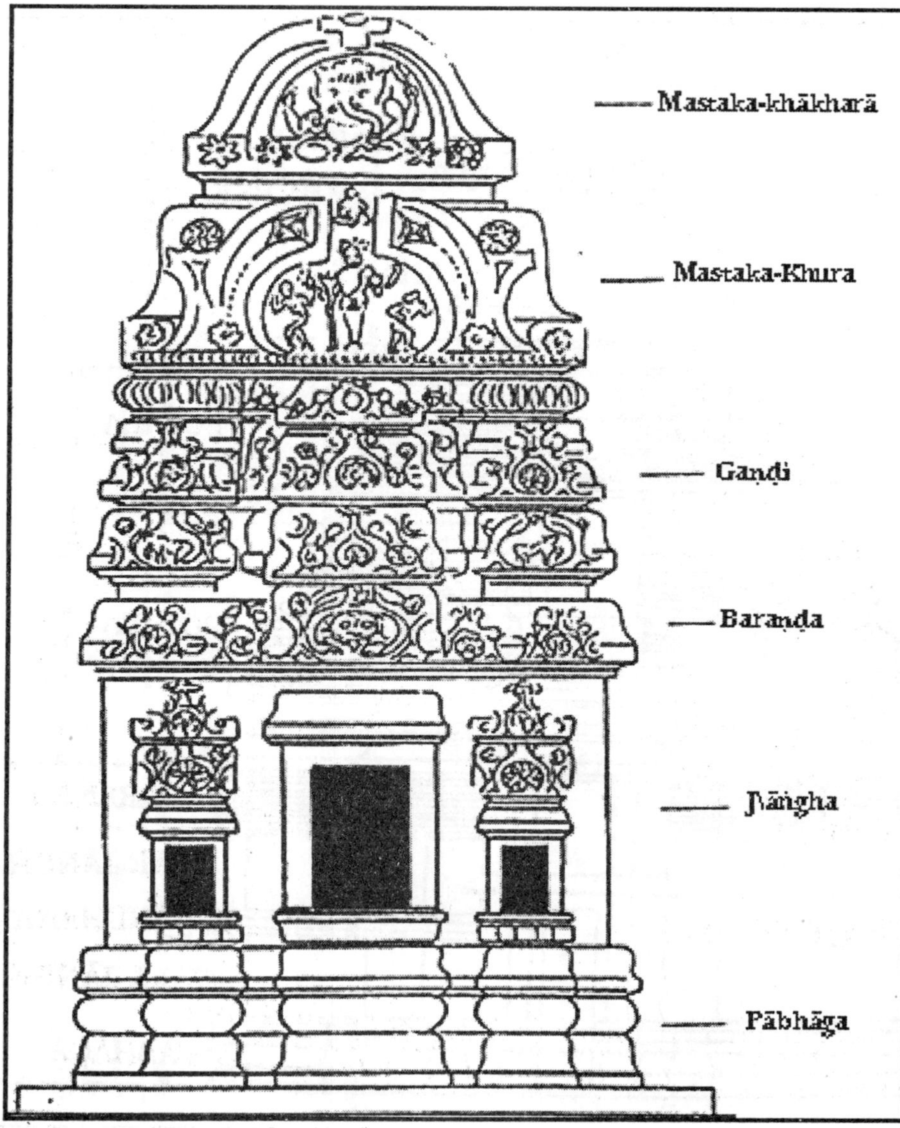

Fig. 3. Elevation of *khākharā deula*

The *anuratha* recesses of the later temples are set with the *vyāla, gaja-vyāla* and *nara-vyāla* in the lower *jāṅgha* and loving couples or *kanyās* in a wide variety of postures in the upper *jāṅgha.*

Fig. 4. *Mastaka* of *khākharā* temple

In some early temples the pillars and pilasters generally flanking the doors, windows or filling the recesses are relieved with figures of *nāga* or *nāgī* in ascending or deseeding mode. They are generally depicted in human form from waist upwards and serpentine below the waist with a canopy of serpent hoods over the head. The prominence given to the *nāga* pillars may be recognized as a special feature of Orissan temple for they are almost unknown elsewhere.[12]

The grill design window in the early temples are often relieved with the cult images or other secular figures while the balusters in the balustrade window of the later temples are generally carved with figures of indolent maiden as prescribed by *Śilpa Prakāśa.*[13]

On the door way we four-armed *dvārapālas* carved at the base of the jamb. The jamb is decorated with three or four bands of carving which include scrollwork, rope hands, gourd bands, *gelabai,* lotus petal bands and occasionally panels of *mithunas.* On some temples *nāga* figures and river goddesses Gaṅgā and Yamunā stand beyond the. The lintel image varies, however, the most common figure is that of Gajalakṣmī. The *graha* panel on early temples contains the figures of eight *grahas* while the panel on the later temples display the figures of nine *grahas.*

Vajra-mastakas appear at the base the *rāhā-pagas* of the *śikhara,* this design being more elaborate on the frontal *rāhā.* They are also seen on the *mukhaśālā* roof above the central projections and entrance door.

Kīrttimukhas or the face of glory representing the head of a lion like creature with four strands of pearls issuing from the mouth are usually found at the top of the *vajra-mastaka* decorating the *rāhā-paga.* It also appears at the top of the *bho* arch.

Bhāra-vāhakas seated in *kakkutāsana,* normally depicted in pairs generally appears at the top of the pilasters. *Pūrṇa ghaṭas* or vase overflowing with foliage decorating the base and the top of the pilasters are prominent in earlier temples.

Lions crouching on elephants decorate the *śikhara* and sometimes the base of the *nāga*-pilasters. *Udyatā* lion appears on the *śikhara* of the later temples. Lion with two hind parts and *beki-bhairava* decorate the *beki.*

The *vajra-mastakas* and all arches on the wall are outlined with decorative dots. *Jhara-vali* or rows of pendants are seen along the dotted arch. *Jālī* panels are to be seen alternating with vases, pilasters, couples and occasionally with *bhāra-vāhakas.*

Floral motifs like bands of lotus petals and bands of rosette are seen as boarders to the various levels of the *bāḍa* and the *śikhara*.

Various types of leafy scrolls decorate the pillars and pilasters. In later temples they also decorate the various levels of the *śikhara*. The *gelabai* scroll with an undulating stem within the curves of which are placed tiny figures climbing up the stem occurs in all the temples from the earliest to the latest. Scrolls in the form of creepers with full or half medallions enclosing leaf designs and animal figures occur on later temples.

Human being in domestic scenes, acrobatic feats, ritualistic worship, relaxing in music, listening to a teacher fighting the enemy or on procession and birds, beasts, aquatic animals, composite and mythological figures are also seen decorating the walls of the temple. Panels depicting scenes from the *Mahābhārata* and the *Rāmāyaṇa* also appear on some temples.

References

1. Soma Chand, *Orissa Review*, July 2005, p. 49.
2. R.P. Mohapatra, "Traditions in Architecture", *Art Traditions of Orissa*, Orissa Sahitya Akademi, Bhubaneswar, 1983, p. 14.
3. *Ibid.*
4. N.K. Bose, *Canons of Orissan Architecture*, Calcutta, 1982, p. 122.
5. *Ibid.* p. 122.
6. T.E. Donaldson, *Hindu Temple Art of Orissa*, vol. II, Leiden, 1987, p. 769.
7. N.K. Bose, *op. cit.*, p. 79.
8. Debala Mitra, *Bhubaneswar*, New Delhi, 1961, p. 19.
9. *Ibid.*, pp. 19-20.
10. Vidya Dehejia, *Early Stone Temples in Orissa*, New Delhi, 1979, p. 23.
11. Stella Kramrisch, "The Walls of Orissan Temples", *J.I.S.O.A.*, vol. XV, 1947, pp. 186-194.
12. Vidya Dehejia, *op. cit.*, p. 23.
13. *Śilpa Prakāśa*, I, 365-375, pp. 43f.

Chapter IV

Temple Building Activities

Temples of the Śailodbhava Period

The earliest standing temples of Orissa, judged from of the *śikhara* and the style of decoration, are not earlier than the sixth century CE. Thus it is difficult to determine the shape of the temples in their initial and formative stage. In the Hāthigumphā inscription (first century BCE) Khāravela is described as the "repairer of all shrines of gods"[1] (*seva-devayatana-śaṅkara-karako*), but there is no evidence to ascertain their architectural significance. On the top of the Udayagiri hill the remains of an apsidal structure[2] have been excavated, but from its foundation and other traces it is difficult to determine the date and form of this religious edifice. Some architectural fragments and detached sculptures, representing *Yakṣa* and *Nāga* images[3] belonging to the early centuries of the Christian era have been found, but those few relics do not give any precise idea about the type of religious building to which they belonged.

During the Gupta period some temples were erected and of them few have survived, but in Orissa as yet no specimen of this epoch has been brought to light. A long piece of stone possibly the lintel of a temple, has been collected from the

Bhadrakālī temple near Bhadrak, and bears an inscription of one Mahārāja Śrī Gaṇa.[4] The paleography suggests that it belongs to the latter half of the third century CE and from this it seems possible that there was a temple which was erected by the said king. Another stone inscription engraved below an image of *Naṭarāja*, discovered in the village of Asanpat (Keonjhar district) refers to the construction of a temple by Mahārāja Śatrubhañja[5], who may be assigned to the third or fourth century CE on the basis of the paleography of the inscription. However, except for this image of Naṭarāja, and "old bricks lying scattered in an area about of an acre of land"[6] nothing remains from which we can reconstruct the form of the original temple. Two little shrines, one dedicated to Durgā on the top of a hill near Patia, Cuttack district and the other the Nīlakaṇṭheśvara shrine on the top of Jagamanda hill near the village Padmapur (Koraput district), are generally assigned to the Gupta period. There is another such temple on the Mahendragiri. Except for the use of big blocks of stone which recalls the practice followed in one Gupta temple at Kund (district Jabalpur)[7], we do not find the usual Gupta characteristics to be certain of their dates. An inscription[8] on the Nīlakaṇṭheśvara temple from its paleography suggests that it could not have been built later than seventh century CE.

The early series of temples were probably erected during the period of the Śailodbhava kings who ruled from the middle of the sixth century till the first half of the eighth century CE. In the inscriptions, Koṅgoḍa[9], the present Ganjam-Puri districts, is described as the territory ruled by the Śailodbhavas. The Śailodbhava kings professed Śaivism, and under them a vast religious and cultural resurgence took placed which were symbolized by the performance of *aśvamedha* and *vājapeya* sacrifices. During the rule of the Śailodbhavas some of the early temples of Bhubaneswar, like Śatrughneśvara, Paraśurāmeśvara and Svarṇajaleśvara, were erected at Bhubaneswar.

The temples of this early phase show certain characteristics. The *tri-ratha* form, a cube of three divisions, a *pābhāga* of three mouldings, the *baraṇḍa* terminating in a recessed *kanti*, the gradual curvature and stunted form of the *śikhara* unburdened by any *aṅga-śikhara*, and the absence of *dopichhā* lions below the *āmalakaśilā* are some of the main features of the early type. In the early temple, the sculptures appear in low relief and "encrusted on the surface of stone."[10] The absence of Ketu among the *grahas* (planets) is another characteristic of the early group. Again the earlier temples can be divided into two groups, those without *jagamohana* and those having a rectangular *jagamohana* with terraced roof. But on grounds of style these two groups are close and they can be regarded as different expression of one movement. The prominent temples of this period are Bhārateśvara, Lakṣmaṇeśvara and Śatrughneśvara temples of Bhubaneswar. Besides, the temples of Paraśurāmeśvara and Svarṇajaleśvara of Bhubaneswar are also the creation of the Śailodbhava period.

Temples of the Bhauma-Kara Period

The Bhauma-Karas ruled for sometime as close contemporaries of the Śailodbhavas and later on supplanted them. They ruled from the middle of the eighth century to the first quarter of the tenth century CE. During this period several minor dynasties came into existence and they appear to have first ruled as vassals of the Bhauma-Karas but later they wielded considerably power. Of these, a Bhañja family ruled in the Mayurbhanj-Keonjhar region, with headquarters at Khiching, another Bhañja family ruled over Athamallick-Baud region with their capital at Dhritipur, the Śulkis ruled over Kodālaka-*maṇḍala* (comprising Talcher, Dhenkanal area) and the Nanda ruled over Airāvatta-*maṇḍala* (Narsinghpur, Hindol, Angul areas).

The temples that were erected in different parts of Orissa during these centuries, though cannot be definitely ascribed to any one of the Bhauma rulers or their feudatories, belong to their period. The first three rulers of the Bhauma family were Buddhists and it appears that during their period Lalitagiri, Udayagiri and Ratnagiri developed as great centers of Buddhist art. The later Kara kings professed Śaivism and Śākta cults. Their capital was situated somewhere near Jajpur. The Haṁseśvara temple at Jajpur can be definitely attributed to the Bhauma epoch on the basis of an inscription.[11]

The temples of the Bhauma period are not essentially different from the early series, but they represent the continuation and development of the temple building tradition. The persistence of the traditions of the past dynasty as well as the progress of the style are evident from some important temples of the period such as Śiśireśvara temple of Bhubaneswar, Mārkaṇḍeśvara temple of Bhubaneswar, Nīlamādhava and Sidheśvara temples at Gandharadi of Baud, Bhṛṅgeśvara temple at Bajrakot and

Kanakeśvara temple at Kualo of Dhenkanal, Manikeśvara temple at Śukleśvara of Cuttack and Khiching temple of Mayurbhanja, etc.

Taken as whole the period of the Bhauma-Karas was a creative one in the sphere of art and architecture. The temples have many things in common with those belonging to the earlier phase, but the development of the style can also be seen. For example the rectangular *jagamohana* of the earlier times continues, but a distinct advance over the older design is introduced by building its roof on the cantilever principle, then, at some later stage, this feature is discontinued and we find only the *deula* without feature is discontinued and we find only the *deula* without any *jagamohana.* The elevation of the *deula* is somewhat similar to the earlier type, but, as the Kanakeśvara temple testifies, attempts were made to increase its height. The sculptures of the period are no longer treated in low relief, but become bold and impressive. As the style progresses there are reasons to infer that possibly a *jagamohana* of the pyramidal form was also invented, to match the tall *deula.*

Temples of the Somavaṁśī Period

The Somavaṁśīs, who succeeded the Bhauma-karas, came from South Kosala, but they did not introduce any unfamiliar line of development in art and architecture. When they were ruling in western Orissa at the beginning of their career the inspiration in building activities possibly came from central India. The Someśvara temple[12] at Ranipur Jharial (District Bolangir) was built by an Āchārya of the Mattamayur school of Śaivism, named Gaṅgan Śiva whose inscription was found on the lintel of the temple.[13] The temple has been assigned to the middle of the ninth century CE as Gaṅgan Śiva is taken to be as Vyoma Śiva mentioned in an inscription at Ranod (Madhya Pradesh). This temple, as well as another Vaiṣṇavite brick temple of the place, is a development of the temple style of Sirpur. The Kosaleśvara temple at Baidyanath, a village in Sonepur P.S. of Bolangir District, on the bank of the Tel River belongs to the Somavaṁśī period.[14] The original *deula* has disappeared and a modern temple has been erected in its place but the original pillared *Jagamohana* still stands in a dilapidated condition. This *Jagamohana* is different from the typical *Jagamohana* of Orissa for it has lateral transepts and large sculptures in the interior.[15] This evidence suggests that when the Somavaṁśīs were ruling in the upper Mahānadī valley, comprising the Sonepur and Bolangir regions, there was some central Indian influence on the temple architecture, but as they conquered Utkala and came down to the coastal region, as heirs to the heritage of the Bhaumas, they strengthened the traditional temple style. Under their patronage the typical Kaliṅga style assumed its final shape and became distinct inform and technique. The *Jagamohana* became an inseparable element of the temple, and leaving behind a phase when it was rectangular with a terraced roof, it emerged as a well formed *pīḍha deula* with *pīḍhas* arranged in continuous succession or in tiers. As the shape of *Jagamohana* was in the process of being standardized, its lattice-windows are replaced by balustrade windows, which served the model for the succeeding centuries. The *deula* also came to possess a soaring quality and majesty not known in the preceding phase. Previously, the form of the *śikhara* was so thick and stunted that it possessed certain heaviness, but now, in the Somavaṁśī period, it had grown into a form of a great beauty, light and rhythmic in its treatment. The projections of the *deula* are not shallow and buttress-like, as is the case with the temples of the earlier epochs, but are well-developed and by their recesses they produce a charming effect in light and shade. Often the *gaṇḍi* was embellished with *aṅga-śikharas,* and these miniature temples, diminishing in size as they rise to the peak, added to the grandeur and ascent of the *śikhara.* Another innovation of the period was the projecting lion from the *rāhā,* with either a *kīrttimukha* or an elephant under it, the latter forming the *Gajasiṁha* motif so popular in Orissan art. The *āmalakaśilā* is supported by *deula chāriṇīs, dopichhā*-lions at the corners and seated divinities, according to the taste of builders. These elements were not known previously. In this period the *bāḍa* is divided into five segments, *pābhāga, jāṅgha, bandhana,* upper *jāṅgha* and *baraṇḍa* which are an advance over the *tiraṅga bāḍa* of the preceding phase. Now, we also find *pañcha-kama-pābhāga-pada, kumbha, pata, kāni vasanta.* The recessed *kanti* of the earlier epoch also disappears and gives place a band of mouldings which demarcate the *bāḍa* from the *gaṇḍi.* In the *bāḍa* we also notice the introduction of structural motifs, locally known as *pīḍha-muṇḍī, khākharā-muṇḍī* and *vajra-muṇḍī.* The sculptures of the period are excellent in their plasticity and modeling, and include non-iconic female figures. The technique of modeling the figures in alto-relievo is also another new development. In the iconography of the cult deities new elements were introduced. The addition of Ketu to the list of planets become permanent and the *Navagraha* also became an indispensable feature in later times.

Thus, a number of new features were introduced in this period. These elements, however, are not found in all the temples of the Somavaṁśī period. The monument built during the early period of their rule; possess maximum features common to the temples of the preceding dynasty but the temples belonging to the developed phase, Liṅgarāja and Brahmeśvara, have all the fundamental characteristics of the Kaliṅga architecture. Some important temples like the Pañchapāṇḍava temple at Jaluka of Cuttack, Mukteśvara temple and Rājarānī temple of Bhubaneswar, etc. bear the testimony of this period.

Temples of the Gaṅga Period

After the Somavaṁśīs, the Gaṅgas became master of Orissa and during their long rule (1112-1435 CE) a number of beautiful temples were built, of which only a few can be dated with any amount of certainty. During the period great and small temples were built by kings (Chodagaṅga Deva and Narasiṁha I built Jagannātha and Konark temple respectively), members of the royal family, (Chandra Devī, the daughter of Anaṅgabhīma III built Ananta Vāsudeva temple at Bhubaneswar, Svapneśvara, brother-in-law of Gaṅga ruler Rājarāja built Megheśvara temple), officers of the realm (Viṣṇu the minster of Anaṅgabhīma III built Chateśvara temple) and vassals (Sri Vaidyānatha built the Sobhaneśvara temple at Niali). The vigorous temple building activities were not confined to a few religious centers like Puri, Bhubaneswar and Konark, but some of the temples can still be seen in small towns or even in insignificant villages. These fine series of temples demonstrate the fallacy of the statement that after Somavaṁśī period, except for Konark, "the story of the Orissan art became a tale of degeneration and decadence."[16]

Before coming to Orissa, the Gaṅga rulers had their capital at Mukhaliṅgam. The temple architecture that developed under their patronage is best exemplified by the temples of Madhukeśvara (possibly built by Gaṅga King Madhukamarṇava), Bhīmeśvara (in all likelihood constructed by Aniyakabhīma Vajrahast, for the temple is also called Aniyaṅkabhīmeśvara temple), and the Someśvara temple. But when the Gaṅga kings came to Orissa, and transferred their capital to Cuttack, they developed the brilliant temple building tradition inherited from the Somavaṁśī period. The temples erected in Orissa are very different in style from the temples at Mukhalingam[17] which represent the early phase of eastern Gaṅga temple architecture.

The temples of the Gaṅga period, are not completely different from those of the Somavaṁśīs. On the other hand, Somavaṁśī temples like the Liṅgarāja and Brahmeśvara served as the models for the Gaṅga builders. Though they continued the tradition, they made certain improvements and introduced certain new elements. During the period of their rule, towards the thirteenth century, after a long process of evolution, the style attained its fulfillment and finality.

Before discussing the individual temples to show the stages in the evolution of the style, the new elements introduced during the Gaṅga period may be mentioned at the outset in order to dispel the misconception that "the artist of the Gaṅga dynasty was no more capable of conceiving a new idea and courageous enough to be a novel experiment".[18]

The Gaṅga temples rarely raise abruptly from the ground as for example the Buddhanātha temple at Garudi panchana; they usually stand on raised platforms. Though they reproduce the basic features as regards plan and elevation, the distinct development of the design can be marked in the *Saptaratha* plan. Though the ground plan of the *deula* remains square, externally the well-developed *pagas*, by their recesses, confer on the temple a circular appearance and this presents a pleasing contrast to the *Jagamohana* with its pyramidal roof. In addition to these two structures, in the more important temples the *Naṭa mandira* was added and being lower than the *Jagamohana* the eye was led from the former to the latter, and finally to the *śikhara* of the *deula* which was dominates the surroundings. The provision of porches or subsidiary temples in front of the *pārśva-devatā* is an altogether new feature. The side structures for the *pārśva-devatās* of the Liṅgarāja temple, in their present clumsy form are obviously later additions. Thus the important temple of the Gaṅga period no longer consists of only a *deula* and a *Jagamohana*, but with its side structures and frontal adjuncts represents a temple complex. The *vāhanastambhas*, are another notable feature of Gaṅga temples. In Śiva temples the bulls, in Viṣṇu temples *Garuḍa*, in a Sūrya temple *Aruṇa* surmount the pillar placed in front of the temple. At the Liṅgarāja temple, the *vāhanastambha*, carrying both the bull and Garuḍa, indicates the religious syncretism of the shrine. The appearance of the consorts of the *dikpālas* on the upper *jāṅgha* of the temple is another new development of the period. This practices, however, has not become well established by the close of twelfth century for the main temple of the Megheśvara at Bhubaneswar or the Sobhaneśvara temple at Niali do not possess female counterparts of the *dikpālas* on the upper *jāṅgha* of the *bāḍa*. The Chateśvara temple at Kisenpur, built by Viṣṇu, the minister of Anaṅgabhīma III (1206-1238), shows that the depiction of consorts of the *dikpālas* had by them become an established practice. On this criterion the temples of the Gaṅga period can be divided into two groups: early and late, the latter class distinguished by *dikpālas* with their consorts. Leaving behind restraint and simplicity of decoration, the elaborately carved surface of the temple swells with a new vigour. The temples are distinguished by wonderful richness and prodigality of details not found previously. Among the important decorative devices are diamond cuttings of great beauty, and scrolls enclosing animals, birds, etc., carved in the manner peculiar to this epoch. The architectural features of the Gaṅga period are exhibited in the temples of Lord Jagannātha, Buddhanātha, Gopinātha, Somanātha, Chaṇḍeśvara, etc. along with the Sun temple of Konark and Ananta Vāsudeva temple of Bhubaneswar.

Temples of the Gajapati Period and After

The Gajapati period, which followed that of the Gaṅgas was glorious in the political field, but no development is to be noticed in the sphere of temple building activities and art. A few temples were erected in this period, but they pale into insignificance before those of the earlier ages. As a representative specimen we may cite the Pāpanāśinī temple of Bhubaneswar, which evidently belongs to the reign of Kapilendra Deva (1435-1467 CE) for an inscription referring to this king, has been discovered on this wall.[19] Except for a panel depicting an elephant procession and an elegant image of Naṭarāja, the surviving sculptures which consists of decorative female figures, are of inferior workmanship. The Kapileśvara temple near Bhubaneswar consisting of *deula*, *jagamohana*, *naṭa mandira* and *bhōgamaṇḍapa*, also belongs to the reign of Kapilendra Deva according to traditions. A comparison of its sculptures and decorations with those of the Ananta Vāsudeva group, presents a contrast showing the decline of creative art. The Jagannātha temple at Gopinathpur (Cuttack district) also belonged to the same reign. According to an inscription found on the compound wall of the temple, it was constructed by a minister of Kapilendra Deva named Vāmadeva.[20]

During the reign of Gajapati Puruṣottama Deva (1467-1497 CE) some temples were built. According to tradition he built the Sundara Mādhava temple at Purusottampur in the Ganjam district. The *bhōgamaṇḍapa* of the Jagannātha temple at Puri, according to the *Madalapañjī*, was also constructed by this king. The ornamentation of the high platform and the *bāḍa* of the *bhōgamaṇḍapa* are not of very high order. Among the chlorite sculptures, pieces depicting the king and attendants in a pleasure boat, the king on a wing and the king worshiping the Śiva-*liṅga*, Durgā and Jagannātha, recall similar panels at Konark and indicate the profound influence exercised by its sculpture. There is no evidence to suggest that these cravings were actually brought from Konark; moreover they differ in size, workmanship and details of composition. Probably, they are imitations of their earlier prototypes. The erotic sculptures made of chlorite, to be found on this structure, reveal the force of convention even in the hall of offering of a major Vaiṣṇavite shrine.

The Varāha temple at Jajpur, according to the traditions of the *Madalapañjī* and *Jagannātha Kaifiyat*, was constructed by the Gajapati King Pratāprudradeva. But, except for a few isolated sculptures of comparative better workmanship, there is nothing outstanding about it.

In the subsequent centuries several temples were erected under the patronage of the local kings and by the collective endeavor of the people. Some of them closely follow the traditional pattern in the treatment of the *vimāna* and other structures but they possess no great artistic value.

Several factors contributed to the steady decline of artistic activities in this part of India. By the time of the Gaṅga period, the important religious centers of Orissa like Puri, Konark, Bhubaneswar and Jajpur came to possess numerous temples. Since, the number and sanctity of the *kṣetras* remained constant according to the *Purāṇas* and old temples could not be deliberately razed to the ground, this left little scope for building temples.

The repeated Musilm invasions created political insecurity which had its impact on the temple building activities. Dr R.C. Majumdar made a plausible suggestion that "the progress of temple architecture was in inverse ratio to the establishment of effective Muslim authority in particular region in India".[3] In case of Orissa, this seems to be true. After Narasiṁha I's successful wars against Muslim rulers of Bengal there was no great Muslim invasion on Orissa throughout the thirteenth century and in this century, as we have discussed, there was vigorous temple building activities. During the reign of Bhānudeva III (1352-1378 CE) "The very foundations of the Gaṅga Empire were shaken by the repeated onslaughts of the Muslim".[4] During the Gajapati period Orissan rulers had to fight with the Islamic powers of Bengal and Bahamani kingdoms. After the Gajapatis, the rulers of short-lived Bhoi dynasty came to guide the destiny of Orissa and at least the period of turmoil resulted in the end of independent Hindu rule in 1568. The Mughal rule that followed could not be expected to have contributed to the growth of art in Orissa. Aurangzeb is known to have given a general order for the destruction of Hindu temples from Midnapore to Cuttack. It is needless here to repeat the acts of vandalism of those days. In these circumstances, it is natural that the rulers paid more attention to conserve what have been already built than to construct new temples.

Apart from the effects of Muslim invasions and domination, an examination of the sculptural embellishments on the temples of the later epochs, shows that a process of decadence and inward decay had already started in the realm of art. The products generally are in the nature of cheap imitations of their earlier prototypes, lacking in originality of talent and creative vitality. In the Gaṅga period, the decorative motifs became standardized and their appropriate places were fixed by convention. The division of *pābhāga* into 5 mouldings, *khākharā* and *pīḍha-muṇḍīs* in the *jāṅghas* containing *dikpālas* and their consorts, *gajavidalas* in the recesses of the projections in the lower *jāṅgha*, erotic couples and *kanyās* in the recesses of the upper *jāṅgha*, formed the essential pattern in the treatment of the *bāḍa*. Only a few minor variations are made in the number of *bandhana* and *baraṇḍa* mouldings. These basic features are repeated in all the temples like Chitrakāriṇī, Sari deula, Ananta Vāsudeva, Yameśvara, etc. The artists do not make any significant departure from established practice. Some of the important decorative motifs look alike even though they come from different temples. For example the *gaja-vidala* motif became so standardized, that even in the hands of different artists it possesses little individuality. The motif remains beautiful no doubt, but its form became fixed as though it belonged to the realm of iconography. This is also true of other conventional decorative motifs such as *nāga*, *nāgīs*, *kīrttimukhas*, etc. It is not known for certain, when the extant *Śilpa śāstras* came to be compiled, some of them seem to have been of a very later date.

Whatever may be their value, the codifications and elaborate prescriptions enjoined in those texts must have contributed to curtail the freedom of the artists. The more the artist adhered to these rules, the less he became free to show his talent and materialize his creative ideas. This process could not have been congenial to artists of vision. In these circumstances art became devoid of freshness and vitality and such a stereotyped art could not have continued for long without atrophy. Thus, the decline appears to be due to both external danger and inward decay; the former no doubt accelerated the process of the later. But what remains, in shape of living tradition among the *sthapatis* of Orissa, is really impressive, and it reminds us of the glorious heritage and achievements of their ancestors in the distant past.

References

1. Hāthigumphā inscription vide N.K. Sahu, *History of Orissa*, line-17, vol. I, Bhubaneswar, 1964, p. 404.
2. Debala Mitra, *Udayagiri and Khandagiri*, New Delhi, 1960, pp. 38-39.
3. K.C. Panigrahi, *Archeological Remains at Bhubaneswar*, Orient Longmans, 1961, pp. 207-210.
4. *OHRJ*, vol. I, no. 2, pp. 22-26.
5. A.DAS, Asanpat *OHRJ*, vol. XIII, no. 2 (July 1965), pp. 1ff.
6. *Ibid.*, p.6.
7. *JAS*, vol. VII, 1965 (nos. 1 and 2), pp. 79-81.
8. N. Senapati (ed.), *Orissa District Gazetteers*, Koraput, 1966, pp. 424-25.
9. N.K. Sahoo, *History of Orissa*, vol. I, Cuttack, 1964, pp. 111-113.
10. Stella Kramrisch, *Indian Sculpture in the Philadelphia Museum of Art*, University of Pennsylvania, 1960, p. 50.
11. *E.I.*, vol. XXVIII, p. 180.
12. At Ranipur Jharial J.D. Beglar saw 57 temples when he visited the place. Of these he gives details descriptions of a temple dedicated to the 64 *Yoginīs* and of the Someśvara temple which is the highest temple of the group.
13. *OHRJ*, vol. II, no. 2, pp. 65-75.

14. Someśvara II (first quarter of twelfth century CE) in his Kumārī Simha plates refers to God Vaidyanātha; the temple must have existed before his period.

15. The sculpture treatment of the interior is a feature of the Somavaṁśī period. There is a possibility of this feature being originally inspired by traditions of central India.

16. *OHRJ,* vol. XI, no. I, (1962), p. 49.

17. M. Rama Rao, *The Temples of Kalinga,* Tirupati, 1965, pp. 19-37.

18. *OHRJ,* vol. XI, no. I (1962), p. 49.

19. *JAS,* vol. IV, no. I (1962), pp. 91-92.

20. *Ibid.*

Chapter V

Khākharā Temples

In the annals of temple architecture of India Orissa has the distinction of conceiving religious shrine for enshrining the *Devī* images, canonically known as *khākharā deula.* As mentioned in the *Śilpa* texts there are three types of *khākharā* temples such as *Kosali, Varabhi* (*Vallabhī)* and *Draviḍa*[1] according to *Viṣṇudharamottara Purāṇa*[2] such temples are designed to accommodate either a group of deities or a reclining Viṣṇu.[3] In the Vaitāl *deula,* possibly the earliest surviving *khākharā* temple in Orissa, there are in fact a group of fifteen images including eight *mātṛkās* enshrined within the oblong sanctum. It is quite plausible that temples dedicated to the *mātṛkās* were of the *khākharā* order. Whereas the *bāḍa* of the temple is decorated in the same general manner as that of the *rekhā* order or *pīḍha* order it correspondently undergoes a similar evolution and indirectly influences changes in the *gaṇḍi* of the *khākharā* temples.

According to *Śilpa Prakāśa,* the *yoginī yantra,* which is particular to the *Devī* temple is engraved and worshipped at the base of the *garbhagṛha.* This *yoginī yantra* consists of seven triangles issuing from three points placed at equal distance upon one straight line. This straight line running from north to south is called *raja rekhā,* and the three points represent the three *guṇas* – *sattva, rajasa* and *tamasa* of the seven triangles[4], two belong to *sattva* and *tamasa* each and three amongst which the central and biggest one, belong to *rajas, raja* a clearly preponderant position in this *yantra.* The *guṇas* represent the fundamental tendencies of which the universe is composed. *Sattva,* the upward tendency, rising and aspiring towards purity and light; *tamasa,* inertia, heaviness, the downward pull towards darkness and *raja* the expanding tendency, the activating power behind the two others. They are also assimilated to the three fundamental directions of space, the upward, the downward and the transversal. At the first rupture of the equilibrium, of the *samarasaya* of Śiva and Śakti, these three tendencies, striding as under, represent the first stir of creation. They are also represented as three *bindus* or three *śakti,* viz, *ichhā śakti, jñāna śakti* and *kriyā śakti.*The commentary of *Śrīkrama* to the *Ānandalaharī* says there are three *bindūs,* the first of fire is indicator of *raja guṇa* and Brahma. This is the face of *śakti.* The second and the third are the two breasts which are Viṣṇu and Rudra and indicate *sattva* and *tamasa guṇa.*[5]

This *yoginī yantra* has to be drawn on a rectangular field in the dimensions of the *garbhagṛha.* Here the question arises, why Devī temple has to be rectangular on plan, while Śiva and Viṣṇu temples are based on a square. The procedure followed in establishing this lay-out may give a clue to its meaning to find the outer properties of breadth and length the architect could easily measure out a rectangle of 4 x 3; and then simply divide this into 4 x 3 (12) squares, to obtain the same result that finally emerges from the more complicated follow up operations. The architect is enjoined to draw first a perfect square, and divide the square by two lines vertically into three equal strips, then adds one of these strips to one side of the square and divides the area thus obtained by two horizontal lines. Thus, he obtained the above-mentioned rectangular of 12 (3 x 4) squares. The two central squares (1 x 2) represent the *garbhagṛha,* while the rest is the wall-work up to the *kaṇikā.* One may ask why one should proceed in such a roundabout way. But nothing is without reason and this cumbrous operation may well contain vestiges of the original numeric symbolism that underlies the conception of creation or evolution. The square, by which the operation starts, represents one, the primordial unity resting in itself without dynamic stresses, the one without a second self-contained, all-embracing and motionless. When a creative process sets in, this equilibrium is disrupted; the primordial unity is splitting up, as here the square into three oblong parts. These produce a new part equal to them and thus create a new unit, a rectangle which is no longer self-contained as the original unit, but has a dynamic dimension, one side longer than the other. In the middle of this new unit lies a core of two squares. Two represents the female principle which now works from within and throws out further layers to be added to the central body of the temple through prolongation of the lines containing the central rectangular of the *garbhagṛha*. In the architecture of the *vimāna* these produce the projection of the *rāhā* and the *anuratha*.[6]

Plan

It is found that in contrast to the square plan of the *rekhā* and *pīḍha* temples, the *khākharā deula* is invariably oblong on plan both internally and externally with one of the longer side accommodating a door which faces the deity placed against the opposite wall.

Elevation

As like *rekhā* and *pīḍha* temple, externally, on vertical plane, the sanctum of the *khākharā* temple is divided into the usual divisions like *piṣṭa, bāḍa, gaṇḍi* and *mastaka*. The design of all the divisions expects *mastaka* is same as that of the former two temples. Therefore, the architectural and sculptural descriptions given regarding the *rekhā deual* hold well in this connection.

Bāḍa

It is seen upto the *bāḍa* that the architectural features are same with that of *rekhā* and *pīḍha deula*. But the *bāḍa* of the Vaitāl temple is elegantly carved with shallow pilasters in place of *ratha* projections and divine female figures are enshrined in the niches of these pilasters expect one in which *Ardhanārīśvara* image is placed.

Gaṇḍi

The *gaṇḍi* of *khākharā* temples is consisted of two *bhūmis* as found in the Vaitāl temple at Bhubaneswar. But in temples like Vārāhī at Chaurasi, Gaurī at Bhubaneswar, etc. there is the elimination of standard *bhūmi* divisions crowned by a ribbed *āmla* and *baraṇḍa* though the lowest *bhūmi* serves the purpose of the *baraṇḍa* or the first *bhūmi* of the *gaṇḍi*. The *gaṇḍi* in the longer side is either *pañcharatha* or *saptaratha*. The *gaṇḍi* of this type of temple is decorated like the *gaṇḍi* of *rekhā deula*, while in some temple it is decorated with *khākharā-muṇḍī* designs.

Mastaka

The most distinguishing feature of the *khākharā* temple is its semi-cylindrical barrel vaulted elongated roof[7] which faintly resembles a variety of pumpkin known as *kakhāru* in Oriyā version. The particular variety as Debala Mitra points out is known as *vaita-kakhāru* in the Puri district and *vaitalu* or *vaitāla*, a shortened from of *vaita-kakhāru*, in the Mayurbhanja and Balasore district.[8] It seems the form of the roof is a modified survival of primitive halls with a semi-cylindrical roof resting on a framework of timber or bent split bamboo and having a gable or hemispherical end at either[9] side and ridge along the crest line. Generally, these temples are oblong on plan and thus correspond to the *valabhī* (*bāḍabhi*) variety of *khākharā* described in the *Bhuvana pradīpa*, characterized by a semi cylindrical roof resting on a framework of curved rafter.[10] The door is carved on one of the longer sides. Their decorative programme is conditioned by the oblong plan which is continued throughout the elevation while the shorter sides of the earliest temples; generally have representations of the facades of the upper portion of the barrel-vaulted *chaitya* hall. The cross section all through is however, rectangular.

Sanctum

The interiors of the sanctum are plain. But the *Śilpa* texts are silent as to why the interiors are to be left plain. The interior of the *deula* or sanctum is conceived as the *garbha* or womb of the cosmic being. Probably, in conformity with the idea of *garbha* the walls have been left plain. The plainness is essentially required for the serene and solemn atmosphere for the performance of the rituals of the presiding deity enshrined in the sanctum.

As discussed earlier *khākharā deula* is a distinct order to enshrine Śākta deities. Our survey has yielded the evidence of as many as 19 examples of this order distributed in different parts of Orissa. An account of the *khākharā deula* in there chronological order is given in the forthcoming description.

Vaitāl Temple at Bhubaneswar

The Vaitāl temple, situated in a compound along with Sisireśvara, temple at Bhubaneswar is the earliest example of the *khākharā* order in Orissa (Plate 1). The name Vaitāl is perhaps derived from the word *vetala* or spirit with the help of which the *kāpālikas* and tantrics attained *siddhis.*[11] The temple is dedicated to female principle in her terrific form of Kāpālinī.[12] The Śākta tantric nature of the temple is evident from the *aṣṭamātṛkā* images enshrined within the sanctum, inclusion of Mahiṣamardinī and Pārvatī as *pārśva-devatās* in the exterior decorative programme, exclusion of male deities in the subsidiary *paga* niches, the remains of a *yūpa* in front of the *jagamohana* and the placement of the terrifying Kāpālinī as the presiding deity. The temple is built of sand stone. It is facing towards the east. This temple is one of the most beautiful of all Orissan structures.

Plan

The Vaitāl temple is consisted of a *vimāna* and *jagamohana.* Both are two component parts of the same structure. Both are rectangular on plan. The *viman* is

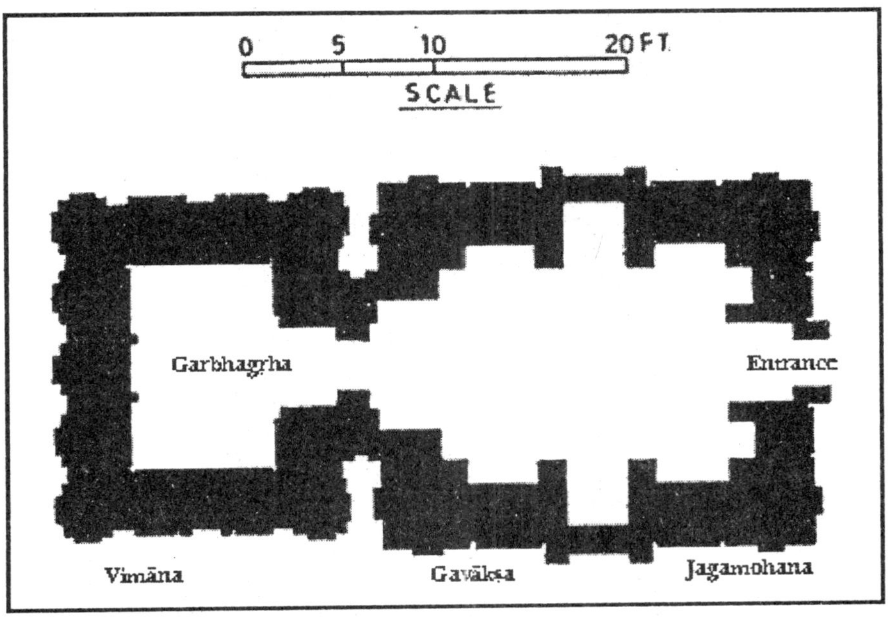

Fig. 5. Ground plan of Vaitāl temple, Bhubaneswar

4.66 m on the shorter side and 5.92 m on the longer side, while the *jagamohana* is 7 m in shorter side and 5.77 m in the longer side. There is a plain *sandhisthala* in between them. The *vimāna* is *pañcharatha* in longer side and *tri-ratha* in shorter side.

Elevation

On elevation the temple is 11.58 m in height. On vertical elevation the *vimāna* has four fold divisions like *piṣṭa, bāḍa, gaṇḍi* and *mastaka* whereas the *jagamohana*

Fig. 6. Elevation of Vaitāl temple

has three fold divisions such as *piṣṭa, bāḍa* and a flat roof. These structures are constructed on a plain and low *piṣṭa* of 20 cm.

Bāḍa

The *bāḍa* or the wall portion of both *vimāna* and *jagamohana* are *triaṅga* in style or have three fold divisions (*triaṅga bāḍa*) such as *pābhāga, jāṅgha* and *baraṇḍa.* The *bāḍa* of the *vimāna* is 4.66 m on the shorter sides and 5.87 m on the longer sides and is *tri-ratha* on plan in the north and south sides with the *kaṇikās* designed as *kumbha-stambhas* with a *vajra-muṇḍī* carved on the centre facet of the shaft.

The *pābhāga* or the foot portion of the temple has four horizontal moulding such as *khūra, kumbha, paṭṭa* and *kani* in succession from bottom to top. The upper two mouldings are ornately decorated with scrollwork.

The *jāṅgha* above the *pābhāga* has single storeyed design. Instead of the *ratha* projections the *bāḍa* has shallow pilasters, all on the same plane and most elegantly designed. It has *tri-ratha* in the northern and southern sides, while *pañcharatha* in the western side. The temple opens in the eastern wall. In the shorter side of the *bāḍa* there are three pilasters like *kaṇikā, rāhā* and *kaṇikā.* The *kaṇikās* on both the sides of the central *rāhā* are designed as a *vajra-muṇḍī.* The shaft is decorated with *vajra-muṇḍī* and the offsets are likewise decorated with *ratikera* scrollwork. An elephant frieze is carved on the *jāṅgha* and aligned with the lions. The flat *kumbha-stambhas* frame the niches. The decorative motifs comprise *pūrṇa-ghaṭa, mithuna,* lotus, other flowers triple-lions and *maliphula phadika.* The niches look like window instead of door (Plate 2).

On the backside there are five such pilasters each crowned by pairs of *vidalas* seated back to back above two carved mouldings. The niches immediately above the *pābhāga* mouldings contain figures of *Ardhanārīśvara* and *nāyikās* (female figures) in different poses. On the two shorter sides, on the north and the south, the decoration of the corner pilaster is exactly the same as those on the back wall. The *nāyikās* are occupying the niches just above the *pābhāga* mouldings wherein placed are the amorous couples. Above these niches there are square panels containing two rampant lions flanking a *kīrttimukha.* Strings of pearls drip down from the mouth of the *kīrttimukha* as well as from the mouth of the rampant lions. This is a unique feature, not found in any other temple of Orissa. These two pilasters on each side are not conceived as independent pilasters and are found supporting the elaborate *vajra-mastakas* on the *gaṇḍi.*

The *baraṇḍa* consists of two projecting mouldings separated by a recess and filled in with various figure motifs, mundane and divine each scene separated from the other by thin pilasters. These scenes are *mithunas,* figures leaning on a staff, standing female figures, inebriated men supported by females, *kāpālikas, liṅga-pūjā* and one representing Śiva begging alms, which combines aspects of *bhikṣāṭanamūrti* and *kaṅkālamūrti* of Śiva.

The font or east facade of the temple was designed in the manner of an entrance portal with flanking *kumbha-stambhas* similar to the short sides though projecting out about 51 cm. The *sandhisthala* of the temple is plain.

Gaṇḍi

The *gaṇḍi* like a truncated *rekhā* terminated at the second *bhūmi* and demarcated by oblong *bhūmi-āmalās.* The *gaṇḍi* in the north and south sides is *tri-ratha* on plan associated with a big *vajra-mastaka,* which consists of two *chaitya*-medallions. The upper medallion is circular and crowned by a *kīrttimukha* with strings of pearls dripping from its mouth to form the borders of the medallions. It contains an image of Lakulīśa in the south side and Hari-Hara in the north. The intervening niche between the pilasters on the south is carved with four-armed standing figure of Pārvatī, and slightly above it are the figures of Śiva and Pārvatī. The corresponding spaces or the northern face have been carved with figures of eight-armed Mahiṣamardinī and four-armed Pārvatī. The *gaṇḍi* in the western side is *pañcharatha* on plan and continued the division of the *jāṅgha.* The east side, *tri-ratha* in design, is dominated by the large projecting *vajra-mastaka,* (above the *jagamohana*). This *vajra-mastaka* is consisting of two *chaitya*-medallions, the upper one housing the image of Naṭarāja and the lower one of rectangular niche housing an image of Sūrya in his chariot. Above the second *bhūmi* there is a large semi-circular member forming the top of the *gaṇḍi.*

Unlike other temples of Orissa its spire is four-sided, which ends in a long ridge set off with three *kalaśa.* The *gaṇḍi* is also four-sided without any projection and butters. The shape is peculiar to the southern Indian *gopuram* or porpillon and nowhere else in northern India been adopted for a temple proper.

Mastaka

Above the *gaṇḍi* there is a small recessed *beki* which is decorated with *pūrṇa-ghaṭa, jālī* motifs and *yakṣa* figures. But the crowning *mastaka* (Plate 3) in the shape of a big *khākharā* is undecorated. The ridgeline along its crest contains three *āmla, khapuri* and *kalaśa* with *triśūla* as finial and probably, on the east or front facade an *udyatā* lion is added later on. The temple is locally known as *tinimuṇḍīā* (three headed) temple.

Fig. 7. *Mastaka* of Vaitāl temple, Bhubaneswar

Sanctum

Unlike the cella of other temples, where light and shade intermingle to create a serene atmosphere, the sanctum of the Vaitāl is intensely dark. Darkness is no doubt of an altogether different ground plan that has been followed in this temple. The seriousness of the awful esoteric rites that were once performed here must have been heightened by the darkness of the cella and by the presence of some images in their most terrific forms. Among the terrific figures carved on the inner wall, occur a Bhairava and Chāmuṇḍā (Kapālī) depicted in the most hideous and terrific form that human imagination can ever conceive. This image might have been another deity of worship for the *kāpālikas,* who took Bhairava to be the creator, protector and destroyer of the world and believed that other gods are subservient to him.

Doorjamb

The doorframe of the sanctum consists of two bands which are decorated with scrollwork, the scroll motifs being the *kuṭilā* and the *gelaba.* A niche is provided at the base of the jambs on each side for the *dvārapālikās*[13] (female door keepers). As it is a *khākharā* temple, dedicated to female goddess, the door keepers are females. They stand in a mirror-image pose with one leg crossed behind the other and the *cauri* holding diagonally across the body, though their eyes are downcast and the pose seemingly placid, they appear stout with energy. These images on the *Vaitāl deula* are better articulated in respect of physical proportion and more refined in details than the earlier temples. The doorframe is flanked on each side by a projecting *kumbha-stambha,* decorated with *ratikera* scrollwork on its shaft.

Jagamohana

The frontal hall or the *jagamohana* measures 7 m by 5.77 m at the base and is a rectangular structure, An unusual feature is the addition of four-miniature *śikhara deula* at each of the four corners. It was probably the first step of the evolution of the temples of *pañchāyatana* plan. The *khapuri* and *kalaśa* of the corner shrine rises above the roof of the *jagamohana.* The rectangular *jagamohana* of the Vaitāl is the last phase in the evolution of the rectangular *jagamohana* in Orissan temple architecture.

The *pābhāga* of these miniature shrines measures 36 cm in height and consists of three plain mouldings. The *jāṅgha* is *triaṅga* in design between the corner *rekhās* with the central *gavākṣa* projection framed by thin pilasters which extended up to the height walls. Both the inner and outer faces of the walls in the porch are devoid of decoration, but the outer faced in the south has a *jail* window.

The narrow door opening on the east end of the *jagamohana* is framed at the side by a thin pilaster incised with *pūrṇa-ghaṭa* at the base and top and *ratikera* scrollwork on its shaft. Due to the sloping eave projecting over the doorway only a thin lintel was there with some obliterated decoration. There is no place for *dvārapālas*. Probably the niches of the unfinished *vajra-muṇḍī* flanking the door were intended to house the *dvārapālas* or river goddesses and the free-standing *nāgas*, now placed inside the *jagamohana*. Probably, they were affixed to the pilasters framing the door. The remains of a *yūpa* are situated in front of the entrance to the *jagamohana*, slightly north of the east-west axis. Two images superimposed one above the other and housed in a shallow niche are carved on the surface facing the door. They are each scated in *dhyānāsana* with both legs firmly locked holding their hands in front of the chest. Probably towards the end of the tenth century CE a small *pīḍha* shrine, its roof supported by four short pillars, was added in front of the door, a few m eastward of the *yūpa*. Within this shrine is a small *chaturamukha* pillar, designed as a miniature *rekhā-deula* with a niche on each side. Enshrined within the niches are Pārvatī, Gaṇeśa, Aja-Ekapāda and Sarasvatī.

Cult Images

The *pārśva-devatās* or the family deities placed in the *rāhā* niches on the north and south sides of the *deula* are Mahiṣamardinī and Pārvatī respectively, whereas the central niche on the longer west side contains an image of Ardhanārīśvara. The image of Mahiṣamardinī (Plate 4) is eight-armed. She holds a shield, a bow and a serpent in her left hands and her right hands hold a sword, a *vajra*, an arrow and a trident which pierced into the left shoulder of the demon. Her major left hand forces back the buffalo-head of the demon and her uplifted right leg is planted on the shoulder near the trident. A similar image is now kept against the wall inside the *jagamohana*. Pārvatī stands in a slightly flexed *tribhaṅga* pose holding a water pot, a trident, a rosary and a *kartri* (chopper) in her four hands. The niches on the entablature above these *pārśva-devatās* are filled in with Hara-Pārvatī on the south and a seated Pārvatī on the north. Here Pārvatī holds a rosary and a *kartri* in her upper hands and a *vija-pūraka* in the lower left hand while the lower right hand is extended in *varada* displaying a lotus mark on the palm. The lower corners of the niche are decorated with a lion and deer. Ardhanārīśvara is depicted standing in a very graceful *tribhaṅga* pose. The deity is four-armed which holds a *vija-pūraka*, a rosary and a flower in three hands and hangs the lower left hand gracefully.

Other important cult images in the *gaṇḍi* of the temple are those of Hari-Hara and Lakulīśa filling the circular *chaitya*-medallions of the *vajra-mastaka* motif on the north and south sides. The image of Hari-Hara is seated with legs crossed holding a rosary and conch in his upper hands. His lower right hand is extended in *varada*, displaying a lotus mark on the palm, while the lower left hand holds a *vija-pūraka*. He is depicted in *ūrdhvaliṅgam* as is Lakulīśa. The later is depicted in *dharmachakra-pravartana-mudrā* with the *lakuta* held against the body with his right arm. He is flanked by four disciples seated on lotus cushions. There is a circular *chaitya*-medallion of the *vajra-mastaka* on the front facade of the *gaṇḍi*, where in a twelve-armed Naṭarāja is depicted; Nandī also appears between his legs while he holds the serpent near his right hip. The lower rectangular niche of the *vajra-mastaka* is decorated with an image of Sūrya. He is depicted in the mid-thigh up pose riding his chariot. He holds two long stemmed lotus rosettes in the traditional manner. He is flanked by Uṣa and Pratyūṣa in the act of shooting arrows. A diminutive Aruṇa is seated in front holding the reins of the seven horses of the chariot.

Decorative Motifs and Sculptures

In contrast to the eerie atmosphere of the dark interior, which is required for the type of rituals taking place here, the exterior walls of the sanctum are one of resplendent beauty; decorated by beautiful non-cultic females and meandering creepers. The decoration of the *jāṅgha*, particularly, seems to be intended as homage to woman. The western facade in particular, is one of the greatest testimonies of the sanctification and apotheosis of woman created by the Indian artist. Four female figures are placed in niche flanking the central image of Ardhanārīśvara, feminine in its graceful curves. The female figures, enticing and seductive in pose, are represented in the daily activities associated with woman and, who naturally ever conscious of their charms lost in self-absorption. All of the figures are graceful in their appearance and relaxed in pose, generally crossing the left leg behind the right. They are all bejeweled in a manner which tends to emphasize their ample charms. Their softness is emphasized by the warm hue of the reddish-white sandstone and by the lush creepers, crisply etched decorating the jambs and offsets framing the niches which act as a foil to the curves of the female form. These females are not specific goddesses but *alasta-kanyās* as they are deified however, are known by their haloes and their exalted position on the temple walls.[14]

In terms of execution, the figures are characterized by as soft plasticity of modeling, delicacy of features and perfect equipoise strangely reminiscent of the classical tradition.[15] Regarding the body proportions, they are perhaps perfect from a classical standpoint, as may be created by the Orissan sculptor. They brought a harmony of body parts unrealised by the rather squat figures of the earlier temples and are lithe in contrast to the earthiness of the female figures on the later temples. In terms of three-dimensional volumes they are slightly flat. This treatment is further stressed by their confinement within niches in the Orissan tradition. Though somewhat aloof, betraying no signs of emotion and isolated within their niche, they seem self-content. In regards to sensitivity of modeling they far surpass the best examples on the earlier temples and represent as one of the best creations of the Bhauma-Kara epoch.

For the first time, *mithuna* or amorous images are enshrined in the niches on the *jāṅgha*, formerly meant for Brahmanical deities. Male figures appear on the *jāṅgha* in the company of woman as intimate partners in love, or in the case of Ardhanārīśvara as half-man and half woman and in the Hara-Pārvatī image as the consort of the goddess. The *mithuna* images are also enshrined in the niches of the *kumbha-stambhas* framing the *rāhā*. The *mithuna* images are also appearing in the *baraṇḍa* recess. Generally, the partners stand next to each other with arms embracing the waist or shoulders. In some cases male figures gently caresses the chin of the female figures as display of tender affection. The *mithuna/maithuna* images elsewhere on the temple of the later period are more intimate and the partners become more active. The females often take the initiative, suggesting their, *śakti* nature. In numerous cases while the male seems almost indifferent to the advances of his female consort. She is also very active in the drinking scenes and is likewise represented inebriated.

Of the animal motifs the most numerous are scenes depicting elephants. They often are arranged in a frieze, as on the top course of the *jāṅgha* or on the lower edge of the crowing semi-circular member of the *gaṇḍi*, and are shown in hunting and battle scenes. The largest motifs, however, are heraldic in nature rather than narrative scenes. One of the most interesting of these heraldic images is the triple-lion motif appearing in the shallow niches above the *mithuna* figures on the *kumbha-stambhas* framing the *rāhā*. The motif consisting of adoresed *jāgratas* and a *kīrttimukha* mask is frontally arranged in the centre so that all three-heads are aligned at the top of the panel. This is a more developed iconographic programme than that of the earlier temple. Also more developed is the heraldic motif above the *pūrṇa-ghaṭa* capital of the *kumbha-stambhas*.

The most popular scroll motif is the *ratikera* which decorates the offsets of the *paga* niches and the pilasters flanking the entrance portal of the sanctum. It acts as a marvelous foil to set off the graceful curves of the female forms enshrined within the niches. The foliage generally issues from *pūrṇa-ghaṭa* motifs or the tail of a *haṁsa*. Also popular is the *dhanu ganthis* scroll which appears on a panel above the adoresed *jāgrata* motif. The *haṁsa-latā* scroll popular on earlier temples are now more refined and less chaotic. The carving of scrollwork is generally in neat and crisp, the perpendicular cutting being shallow and the designs adhering close to the surface being typical Orissan style.

Presiding Deity

The dark interior of the sanctum contains fifteen images housed in shallow niches along the base of the wall. Starting from the eastern wall, extending towards the south there is a group of the images of *mastaka*. It is started with Vīrabhadra and ended by Gaṇeśa. The seventh *mastaka*, Chāmuṇḍā occupies a niche in the centre of the western wall of the sanctum. She is larger than all other figures and is the presiding "deity of the temple. She is worshipped in the name of Kapālī and is seated in *ardhaparyaṅka* (Plate 5). She has an emaciated body and has eight arms. Her major right hand holds a *kartri* while her left hand, with elbow supported by the raised left knee, holds a *kapāla* by her chest. Another right hand is in *varada* while others hold a *ḍamaru* and an indistinct object. One of the left arms cradles a *khaṭvāṅga* and places the hand in Carchika with the finger in her gaping mouth. The objects in the other left hands are indistinct. She wears a long garland of skull and a skull medallion is in her coiffure. Her face, with gaping mouth and round eyes protruding from sunken sockets, is fearful. A *Vidyādhara* is there in each upper corner of the back-slab while an owl is perched in the lower left corner. An elephant skin is above her head. Beneath Chāmuṇḍā there is a postrate corpse with a jackal nibbling on its toes. The eighth *mātṛkā* has been tentatively identified as Śivaduti who is invoked in association with the *mātṛkās* in the Mārkaṇḍeya Chaṇḍī.[16] The other *mātṛkās* worshipped inside the sanctum are Brahmāṇī, Kaumārī, Maheśvarī, Vaiṣṇavī, Indrāṇī and Vārāhī. Generally, there are seven mothers in the group, but here is a deviation of the code.

The second group of images begins with a terrifying Bhairava, to the left of Gaṇeśa, who is depicted with sunken belly and wearing a garland of skulls. He is seated in an aggressive posture, resting the weight of his body on the left knee, holding a large cleaver in the right hand and a *kapāla* in his uplifted left hand. The next niche contains a male figure seated in *ardhaparyaṅka* with his uplifted right knee supporting his right hand which holds a lotus. The left hand is resting on the thigh which holds a vase. He may be identified with Kubera, as he has a slight pouch. The thirteenth niche is filled in with a hoar-headed male deity, the male counterpart of Vārāhī, holding a *kuṭhāra* and a *kapāla* of the last two niches one is filled in by a seated figure with a canopy of seven serpent hoods.[17] The same is identified by K.C. Panigrahi as Amoghasiddha, but according to T.E. Donaldson more likely as a *nāga* king and *Gajāsurasaṁhāra-mūrti*. In the later one Śiva is presented with a sunken belly in the pose of killing Gajāsura with a knife Besides these images, there is also a *vajra-mastaka* design on the back wall above Chāmuṇḍā. It is decorated with an image of Gajalakṣmī on the lintel and the *chaitya*-medallion is filled with the image of Hara-Pārvatī in which Śiva is playing on the *vina*.

The images to the left of Gaṇeśa are quite terrifying and thus testify the *tantric* nature of the shrine. The association of Śakti with Bhairava, the terrific aspect of Śiva, is quite old and the *pīṭha* idea narrated in the story of Daksa's sacrifice is tantric in nature. Accordingly, Śiva assumed the forms of many Bhairavas who settled in the vicinity where the severed body parts of Sati were scattered (*Śākta pīṭhas*) to keep watch over them.[18] That human sacrifice formed a part of the ritual in the Vaitāl *deula*, as suggested by the frequent representations of uplifted knives and skull bowls (*kapālas*), is further evident by the remains of a *yūpa* in front of the *jagamohana* as mentioned above. The *tantric* nature of the *Sapta Mātṛkās* is known as indicated from an inscription found in the village of Gangadhar (Jhalwar). Madhya Pradesh, where mention is made of the erection of the terrible abode of the divine mothers in which *dakinis* utter loud and tremendous shouts in carrying out the matic (*tantric*) rites of their religion.[19] The above discussion thus, shows Vaitāl as a shrine of *kāpālikas.*

Stylistically, this temple is assigned to last quarter of eighth century CE. Palaeographical evidence, in the form of a short inscription incised on the outer lace of the wall or the *jagamohana,* on the east side near the right door jamb, likewise suggests a late eighth century date.[20] This interruption may have been the result of a foreign invasion, such as referred to in the *Madalapañjī,* which K.C. Panigrahi interprets as the Rāṣṭrakūṭa invasion under Govinda III recorded in the Sanjan Plates of Amoghavarṣa[21] that took place during the reign of Subhakara I between 805 and 814 CE.

Though this is the earliest extant *khākharā* temple in the state, both architecturally and sculpturally it shows considerable advancement.

Durgā Temple at Baideśvara

It is a small Durgā temple situated near the village Baideswar on the south bank of the river Mahānadī in Cuttack district (Plate 6). It stands at the foot of a hillock. The hillock on the other hand is crowned by another temple of comparable date known as Rāmanātha temple. The Siṁhanātha Śiva temple in the Siṁhanātha Island of the Mahānadī is not far away from this site. The temple is made of khandolite stone and faced the west.

Plan

On plan the temple has a sanctum and a *jagamohona.* The sanctum is rectangular measuring 1.49 m by 2.7 m. The *jagamohana* or the frontal hall is also rectangular measuring 3.60 m by 3.77 m. There are also traces of an enclosure wall all around the temple.

Elevation

On elevation this temple (Plate 7) has four divisions from bottom to top viz.

piṣṭa, bāḍa, gaṇḍi and *mastaka.* The height of the temple is 3.40 m. The temple is resting on a low *piṣṭa.*

Bāḍa

The *bāḍa* of this temple has three divisions such as *pābhāga, jāṅgha* and *baraṇḍa.* The lowest unit or *pābhāga* is consisted of three plain mouldings like *khūra, kumbha* and a *khūra* shaped *vasanta.*

The *jāṅgha* portion of the *bāḍa* has three vertical segments. If the two flanking projections of the *rāhā* will be consider as two *pagas* then it can be regarded as a *pañcharatha* temple. These projections however, do not continue on the *baraṇḍa* and the *gaṇḍi* divisions of the temple.

The side *pagas* are designed as *vajra-muṇḍīs.* The first element above the *pābhāga* is a *tala-bandhana* of six projecting blocks on the larger side and five on the shorter sides though they have been left without decorations. The crowning *vajra-mastaka* consists of two *chaitya* designs. The *rāhā* niche begins above the *pābhāga* and is crowned by a large eave which extends upto the *baraṇḍa.* The niches to the side deities are provided in the central parts of the three *rathas* of the *jāṅgha.* The *anuratha* is shaped in the form of an ornate *khākharā* miniature, the base mouldings or which are decorated by lotus petals, lion and elephant figures. The niches of these *khākharā* miniatures at some places bear relief of figures. In the western niche of the north side is a Mahiṣamardinī in the attitude of killing the demon with a long spear. The eastern niche of the same side depicts a two-armed female draped in rich costumes. An attendant standing on the backside of the main figure holds an umbrella over the later. In the northern niche of the eastern side is placed a four-armed Ajaikapāda holding a vase, a *triśūla* and a rosary in three hands and the remaining one in broken condition. The southern niche of this side has placed the image of the two-armed Kārttikeya in *samapada* pose. He wears the *śikhaṇḍaka* coiffure of two locks. His left hand though rests on the thigh; the right hand holds a *mātuluṅga.* On the south side is seen a spear while close to the left foot of the deity is a peacock with a snake in its beak. Gaṇeśa seated in *mahārājalīlāsana* pose on a plain pedestal appears in the eastern niche of the southern side. Three of his available hands display *laḍḍūs,* broken tusk and the hatchet. The western niche of the southern side represents a figure of eight-armed Mahiṣamardinī.

The *baraṇḍa* is consisted of a single projecting *pīḍha* moulding capped by a recess. The moulding is decorated with a band of *raṅganī* scrollwork on its *muhanti* and spaced *chaitya* designs on its sloping face flanked by *haṁsas* or animals seated back to back.

Gaṇḍi

The *gaṇḍi* is *tri-ratha* on the shorter sides and *pañca-ratha* on the longer east side. The west side, with a wider *rāhā* due to the entrance portal, is also *tri-ratha* in design. The *gaṇḍi* consists of a single *bhūmi* with three *baraṇḍis* crowned by an *āmla* on the corners. These *baraṇḍis,* on both the *kaṇikā* and *anuratha,* are decorated with a small *vajra-mastaka* motif. The lower medallion, keyhole in shape, is carved on the lowest *baraṇḍī* and houses various figure motifs, including a standing *Devī,* warrior on a horse, etc. The circular upper medallion links together the top two *baraṇḍīs* and *bāḍa,* begins above the niche eave and obfuscates the *baraṇḍa* division. It projects out from the *baraṇḍīs* of the flanking *pagas* and consists of large horizontal mouldings decorated with a *vajra-mastaka* at the base and *chaitya* designs on the mouldings above. This large medallion at the base, aligned with the *baraṇḍa,* houses an image of the lion mount of the *Devī.* On the west side this design, starting above the entrance, projects up beyond the *bhūmi* division though its ornamentation has not survived. On the north the lower medallion houses two confronting warrior figures.

Above the *bhūmi* division there is a big *khūra* shaped member which does not partake the *paga* division. The long sides of this member are plain. But the *muhanti* is decorated with a *kumbhikā-bandha* and *raṅganī* scroll. The shorter north and south sides are decorated with a large *chaitya* design which functions as the lower medallion of a *vajra-mastaka* motif. The medallion of northern side houses a figure of *Andhakāsuravadhamūrti* (Plate 8) and of the south side contains an image of Aja-Ekapāda.

Mastaka

The *mastaka* above the *khūra* shaped member, separated by a narrow recess, is semi-cylindrical and flattened at the top. The *muhanti* on the longer side is also decorated with the *kumbhikā-bandha* and *raṅganī* scroll. The shorter sides are decorated with a *chaitya* which forms the upper medallion of the *vajra-mastaka* design below. This medallion on the south houses an image of Gaṇeśa while on the north it contains an image of Naṭarāja (dancing form of Śiva). Naṭarāja is eight-armed and represented as *ūrdhvaliṅgam.* The upper part of the image is missing whereas the lower corners of the medallion are occupied by Bhṛṅgī (mount of Śiva) on the right and on the left by a figure of drummer. The left side of the *chaitya* is decorated with an erotic scene in contrast to the lotus rosette appearing in all the other corners of this medallion.

Sanctum

The roof of the sanctum made of four slabs rests over three roughly dressed inconspicuous corbels. There is a closed chamber over the *garbhamuda.* The image Mahiṣamardinī in the sanctum is loosely kept on an irregularly shaped pedestal of two *khūra* shaped mouldings. The spout of the pedestal faces towards the north.

Doorjamb

The temple faces towards the west with the doorjambs accommodated on the projected *rāhā* of western side. Most of its decorations are lost except for the lintel pill which has a meandering vine framing lotus petals and a small *chakra* in the centre flanked by a *haṁsa* on each side. The *chaitya* window of this side contain peacock with pearl string, rows of petalled flowers and bust of Śiva with snake issuing from his ear.

Jagamohana

The *jagamohana* does not exist. But, in front of the door there are the remains of a plinth, measuring 3.60 m by 3.78 m, which is made of khondalite slabs and this suggests the existence of a *jagamohana.*

Cult Images

The niches of the *rāhā-pagas* are all empty while the side *paga* niches on the west, flanking the door were left uncarved. The *paga* niches on the south side contain an image of Gaṇeśa and an eight-armed Mahiṣamardinī with the demon represented in animal form, on the east the enshrined images are Kārttikeya and Aja-Ekapāda.

The niche on the north side contains images of Pārvatī and a second image of Mahiṣamardinī. Kārttikeya is depicted in a standing pose with a *mātuluṅga* on his right hand and his left hand rests on his thigh. To his right is the *śakti* while the peacock, with a serpent in its mouth, occupies the lower left corner. The second Mahiṣamardinī is six-armed who pierces the buffalo-headed demon with a trident. The images are all archaic in nature and squat in body proportions, which suggest that the workshop responsible for the work was not well established and sophisticated. Stylistically, the temple can be assigned to the last part of eighth century CE.

Presiding Deity

The presiding deity of the temple is an eight-armed Mahiṣamardinī image (Plate 9). The image measures 62 cm by 43 cm. She has in her right hands a trident which pierces the head of the demon, who is attempting to escape from the decapitated carcass of the buffalo, a *chakra* plucks down on the head of the demon while remaining ones hold a serpent, a shield and a bow. According to T.E. Donaldson[22] the image is more accomplished than those of the exterior walls and probably dates from the later part of the ninth century possibly when the *jagamohana* was added. In addition to it there are six loose sculptures leaning against the exterior walls. Those are four Viṣṇu images and two Mahiṣamardinī images, one of which is a Mahiṣamardinī in good state of preservation. Nothing can be said definitely about their association. The presence or Viṣṇu images do not confirm to the cultic specification of the Śākta monument. There is a buried pillar in front of the temple which was probably a *yūpa.*

Stylistically, this temple is assigned to later part of eighth century CE. Thus, chronologically this temple can be placed after the Vaitāl *deula.* Though the temple is small in stature, it is beautifully decorated.

Chaṇḍī Temple at Avana

A Chaṇḍī temple is situated at Avana in Balasore district, about 22 km south-east of Bahanagaon near Soro. The temple was built with laterite slabs in *khākharā* design. The temple is small and devoid of decoration except for a plain stringcourse which divides the *jāṅgha* into two storeyes. On plan the temple is rectangular. The lintel of this temple preserves an inscription, which paleographically can be placed in the Bhauma-Kara period, i.e. ninth century.[23]

At present the temple is totally renovated by A.S.I. and it looks like a *pīḍha* order of temple. The temple is 4 m square at the base. The present height of the temple is about 6.38 m. Inside the sanctum it measures 2.40 m square. The temple is painted with red colour. The finial emblem of the temple is a *chakra*. All the *pārśva-devatā* niches are empty. Near this temple a beautiful Lakṣmī-Nārāyaṇa temple is situated.

The presiding deity enshrined in the sanctum is a three-headed, eight-armed, emaciated Chāmuṇḍā seated in *padmāsana* whom the local people worship as Brahmāṇī. The image is in active worship and the heads are covered with paste. Her major left hand is placed near the chin of the centre head and the little finger possibly in the mouth. The arm probably cradles a *khaṭvāṅga*. Similarly, the right hand is also placed near the chin and possibly holds a *kapāla*. The lower right hand is in *varada-mudrā*. The lower left hand is placed at the knee and holds a small fruit. The third set of hands is extended near this lower pair. But the objects of these hands arc indistinct. The objects held in the uplifted back hands are also indistinct. The upper part of the slab is damaged and the pedestal is mostly buried.

Many stone sculptures were unearthed near the temple. This flourishing site of Brahmanical, Jaina and Buddhist antiquities of early medieval period was brought to light during the year 1981. The images include two Mahiṣamardinī, a *Sapta Mātṛkā* panel, Gaṇeśa, Pārvatī, Boddhisattva, Jaina *tīrthaṅkara* and terracotta tablets depicting, Buddhist *dhāraṇīs*. Some seals containing Buddhist *dhāraṇīs* are also found in different places of the village. It seems that in some stage there was a Buddhist *vihāra* at the place, which was subsequently converted to a Brahmanical shrine. These excavated materials including the terracotta seals arc now preserved in a room of the Beabhumi College in the site.

Nārāyaṇī Temple at Dia

Nārāyaṇī temple is situated at Dia in the Nirakarpur Panchayat of the Khurda district. During the Bhauma-Kara period (ninth century CE) a temple of *khākharā* design was got built in the temple complex of Lord Kapileśvara which became famous as Nārāyaṇī temple. It was a small structure with khandolite stones. However, due to the ravages of nature this temple was demolished and a new rectangular modern building was constructed by the local people. Previously, this *khākharā* temple was enshrined with a ferocious Chāmuṇḍā image as the presiding deity and the goddess was worshipped by the Buddhist tantrikas as well as by the Kāpālikas for attainment of spiritual power. At present the modern shrine contains the eight-armed Chāmuṇḍā, the four-armed Vaiṣṇavī and the eighteen-armed Mahiṣāsuramardinī images and the deities are being worshipped as Mahākālī, Mahālakṣmī and Mahāsarasvatī (Plate 10).

The Chāmuṇḍā (Plate 11) sits in *ardhaparyaṅka* pose on the dead body of a man (*Śavārūḍha*) as prescribed in the *Viṣṇudharamottara Purāṇa.* Her main right hand is shown in *varada-mudrā.* Her remaining right hands hold *khaḍga, akṣamālā* and *karti.* One of the left hand cradles trident, the little finger being inserted into the gaping mouth in the *carccika* mode like the Vaitāl Chāmuṇḍā and Paikapada Chāmuṇḍā illustrated by Donaldson. Another left hand with elbow supported by the raised knee holds a *kapāla.* The remaining left hands hold severed head and bell. She wears two garlands of skulls, one around the neck and the other hanging down up to the seat. She has an emaciated body, sagging breasts, gaping mouth and round eyes protruding from sunken sockets. Jackal is seen feasting on a leg of the corpse and an owl sitting on the chest. The image measures 36 x 19 inches. It may belong to late ninth century CE.

Vaiṣṇavī (Plate 12) seated in *padmāsana* holding *śaṅkha* in the back left hand and *chakra* in the back right hand. The main left hand and the main right hand are shown in *abhaya-mudrā* and *varada-mudrā,* respectively. She wears a long *vanamālā* as prescribed in the *Devī Purāṇa* and *Purbākāraṇāgama.* Garuḍa appears at the center of the pedestal. The image conforms to the *Āgamic* description of Vaiṣṇavī.

Another remarkable eighteen-armed Mahiṣāsuramardinī (Plate 13) is affixed to the masonry slab of the Nārāyaṇī temple. This image lacks the animation and force of the earlier image. She plants her uplifted right foot on the rump of the buffalo-carcass. Her major right hand plunges a trident into the chest of the carcass and the major left hand presses down the head of the demon. The uplifted right hand holds a sword over her head. The other hands are represented with the tail of the buffalo, *vajra*, mace, *chakra*, *ḍamaru*, axe, and an arrow plucking from the quiver fixed to her back. The remaining left hands are shown with a goad, shield, bow, pestle, *kapāla*, *nāga-pāśa* choking the neck of the demon and other indistinct objects. The deity wears the standard ornaments like necklace, armlets, wrist-bands, girdle, *patra-kuṇḍala* and a conical head-gear. Her hair is arranged into a bulging knot on the top of her head. The lion gnaws on the tail of the buffalo. The demon is depicted in placing his right foot on the severed head of the buffalo and holds a sword in his right hand. He wears a beaded head gear. This image is carved on a *viśvapadma* pedestal and measures 36 by 24 inches. It may be placed to the late eleventh or early twelfth century CE.

Chaṇḍī Temple at Kishorepur

A Chaṇḍī temple is situated within a laterite compound at Kishorepur in Betnoti police station of Mayurbhanj district, approximately 25 km southeast of Baripada.

The temple is built of laterite and it belongs to the *pañchāyatana* class, having a *deula* and a *jagamohana*. There are four subsidiary shrines (all of *khākharā* style) at four corners of the compound. The main shrine is *pañcharatha* plan. The temple is facing towards the east.

Plan

The *vimāna* is *pañcharatha* and rectangular on plan. At the base it measures 2.79 m by 2.2 m. It is built on a low platform. But the *jagamohana* is square on plan. The subsidiary shrines at the four corners are rectangular on their plan.

Elevation

The temple measures 4.71 m in height. On vertical elevation the temple is divided into four sections viz., *piṣṭa*, *bāḍa*, *gaṇḍi* and *mastaka*. Both *vimāna* and *jagamohana* are built on same platform, which is very low in height.

Bāḍa

Above the *piṣṭa* it has a *triaṅga bāḍa* having three divisions from bottom to top like *pābhāga*, *jāṅgha* and *baraṇḍa*. The *pābhāga* is 80 cm high and it consists of four mouldings like *khūra, kumbha, paṭṭa* and inverted *khūra* (*kani*). The *jāṅgha* is 1.32 m high and are single storeyed. The *rāhā-pagas* are in the shape of a *pīḍha-muṇḍī* with niches for the *pārśva-devatās*.

Gaṇḍi

The *gaṇḍi* is separated from the *bāḍa* by three *khūra*-shaped mouldings of 83 cm height. The *gaṇḍi* is consisted of three courses of stone almost rounded near the top. The central *rāhā* is decorated by a miniature *rekhā* at the back and the roof is of a *khākharā* order on the north and south. The frontal projection prominently extends up to the top of the *kanthi*. The *chaitya* window member is separated from the top most *khūra* shaped *khākharā* by a plain recess. The *gaṇḍi* is separated from the *bāḍa* by three *khūra* shaped mouldings of 83 cm height known as *baraṇḍa*.

Mastaka

The crowning elements are all missing and the *kalaśa* is now in the debris.

Sanctum

The *garbhagṛha* or sanctum is oblong on plan and measures 1.85 m by 1.22 m. The *garbhamuda* is formed by two planes resting on five corbels. A corbelled niche is existed over the doorframe.

Doorjamb

The doorjambs of the temple are plain.

Jagamohana

The *jagamohana* is *tri-ratha* on plan. The *pābhāga* is comprised of three mouldings. The *jāṅgha* is almost plain except the lattice window in the central projection. The *baraṇḍa* is *khūra*-shaped in design. Over the *baraṇḍa* rises the terraced roof in two stages, the recess in between, however, has no clerestory. The interior of the *jagamohana* is square on plan.

Subsidiary Shrine

At the four corners of the main shrine there are four subsidiary shrines of *khākharā* order. All are rectangular and *ekaratha* on plan. On vertical elevation they have four fold divisions like *piṣṭa, bāḍa, gaṇḍi* and *mastaka.* Now, these shrines are in ruinous condition. The *mastaka khākharā* is separated from the *gaṇḍi* by a recess. No *kalaśa* is found at the top of the shrine.

Cult Images

The presiding goddess, a ten-armed Chāmuṇḍā (1.01 m high) is worshipped in the sanctum. She is depicted in her terrific form with round rolling eyes, an open mouth, bulging teeth and fang, emaciated body with visible bones and veins, pendent breasts and shrunken belly. She is found seated in *mahārājalīlāsana* on the back of a prostrate male wearing a set of decorative ornaments. Her *jaṭāmukūṭa* is fashioned with several heads, chopped-off palons and a snake. Of her five right hands the lowest right hand is in *abhaya-mudrā*; the others carry a *kartri,* a sword, a skull and a *ḍamaru.* Of the three extant left hands the lowest is in *varada-mudrā,* the second holds a severed head and a battle-axe. The trident held in one of her hands pierces the body of the postrate figure. Over her head there is the display of an elephant skin.

The images of *pārśva-devatās* have been removed from their original niches. The ithyphallic deity is of 45 cm in height. He is the male counterpart of Chāmuṇḍā and is now worshipped in the residence of a private person of the village. The god emaciated with veins and ribs visible and with a terrible facial expression dances on the back of a postrate male. Of his six hands, the upper most right hand displays a *ḍamaru.* He is provided with a set of well-designed decorative ornaments. He is flanked by a female attendant holding human skull and trident on each side. There is a beaded halo with flaming edge over his head.

Stylistically, the temple is more akin to the Sāvitrī and Gopāliṇī temples at Bhubaneswar on the ground of its square *jagamohana* its date of construction is assigned to ninth century CE.[2]

Mahiṣamardinī Temple at Sergarh

An interesting Mahiṣamardinī temple is situated at Sergarh, about 12 km, south-west of Balasore town (Plate 14). The temple is of *khākharā* order. It is situated in a compound along with four small *rekhā* temples and all of which are built of coarse laterite except for their doorframes which are made of chlorite. The temple is on *pañchāyatana* plan. The Mahiṣamardinī temple here is consisted of the sanctum only. The temple is facing towards the west.

Plan

The temple is rectangular on plan. At the base it measures 2.83 m by 2.22 m. The four subsidiary shrines are square on plan.

Elevation

The temple has four divisions from bottom to top, viz. *pisṭa, bāḍa, gaṇḍi* and *mastaka.* The temple rests on a low platform of three courses of laterite and is of 65 cm in height.

Bāḍa

The bāḍa is *triaṅga* with three fold divisions like *pābhāga, jāṅgha* and *baraṇḍa.* It has five vertical segments or *pañcharatha* in design. The *pābhāga* is of 63 cm in height and consisted of three mouldings like *khūra, kumbha* and an inverted *khūra* or *paṭṭa.* They are joined at the centre of each *paga* by a vertical band but otherwise devoid of ornamentations. The *rāhā-paga* of the *jāṅgha* is carved as a *pīḍha-muṇḍī* while other *pagas* are plain. The *jāṅgha* measures 48 cm in height and is without any decoration. The niches are now empty. The *kaṇikā paga* of the *gaṇḍi* stands to a height of 2.93 m. The *baraṇḍa* above the jāṅgha consists of two simple mouldings.

Gaṇḍi

At present the temple stands to a height of 3.95 m with a part of *gaṇḍi* and without the *mastaka.* It is in a state of ruins. The *gaṇḍi* of the temple is totally plain.

Mastaka

The *mastaka* of the temple is consisted of a *beki*, an *āmalaka*, a *khapūri*, a *kalaśa* and a *dhvaja*.

Sanctum

The sanctum internally measures 1.65 m by 1.21 m. The *garbhamuda* rests on a series of corbels. There is a pedestal inside the sanctum on which a Mahiṣamardinī image is placed. Another image of Mahiṣamardinī is kept against the wall of the left side.

Doorjamb

The doorframe made of chlorite is lavishly carved with two bands of scrollwork, *vanalatā* and *raṅganī*. The *dvārapālas* are housed in their respective niches and the ceiling of the niche is carved with a pentafoil design. The *dvārapālas* assume a mirror image pose. Their uplifted inside hand holds a *kapāla* and the outside hand rests on a staff. Their facial features and body ornamentation are badly damaged. But their hair appears to be piled high on the head in serpent-like coils. The image of Gajalakṣmī is carved in the centre of the lintel. The goddess is seated in *padmāsana* holding a lotus in her left hand while her right hand extends in *varada* as seen on earlier temples.

The most striking feature of the decorative programme is the architrave, which was originally fixed over the doorframe, but now it lies scattered in front of the temple. It is carved as a *chaitya* design with an image of Hara-Pārvatī within its medallion.

Śiva is four-armed and seated in *lalitāsana* on a low couch. His upper hands hold a rosary and a trident while his lower right hand is in *vyākhyāna-mudrā*. His major left hand gently lifts the chin of Pārvatī. Pārvatī is also seated in *lalitāsana* with her right hand placed on Śiva's thigh. The bull and lion mounts appear beneath the couch. Over this *chaitya* medallion there is a panel decorated with a series of the *Sapta Mātṛkās* with Gaṇeśa and Vīrabhadra at the centre. From the proper right the series consists of Chāmuṇḍā, Vārāhī, Kaumārī, Śivānī, Vīrabhadra, Brahmāṇī, Vaiṣṇavī, Indrāṇī and Gaṇeśa. Each figure is housed in a niche and is associated with their usual attributes and respective *vāhanas*, the representation of Vīrabhadra in *lalitāsana* with a heap in the centre of the panel instead of the side is rather unusual. At the end of the series is the four-armed pot-bellied Gaṇeśa, seated in *mahārājalīlāsana*, the elephant headed deity carries in the lower left hand a ball of *laḍḍūkas* on which his trunk is applied, a hatchet in the upper right hand and a rosary in the lower right hand.

Presiding Deity

Inside the sanctum are two loosely placed images of Mahiṣamardinī, neither of which apparently the presiding deity was (Plate 15). The Mahiṣamardinī figure is displayed with a sword, arrow, spear and disc in right hands and shield, bow, snake in left hands. Remaining one hand of the left side is shown pressing the neck of the demon Mahiṣāsura. Lion as conventional mount of the deity is associated with the images. The right foot of Mahiṣamardinī rests on the hind part of the buffalo. None of these two images seem to have adorned the original Devī temple as the pedestal gives a different size. The Mahiṣamardinī image now fixed at the Khajūreśvara temple as *pārśva-devatā*, however, in all probability was the presiding deity of this temple. Along with all attributes held by eight-armed figures, it carries a severed head in one of the left hands and a *vajra* in one of its right ones.

Cult Images

There is a fragmented *navagraha* slab near the temple. The order of the *graha* is reversed, as at Badagaon with Ravi on the proper left in his chariot in the back of Aruṇa the charioteer. The *grahas* are each represented slightly different, rather than posed identically and hold various weapons and attributes. Besides this a four-armed Gaṇeśa image and a seated Manasā figure with canopy of a seven-hooded snake over head are kept inside the sanctum.

Subsidiary Shrines

There are four subsidiary shrines inside the temple complex of Mahiṣamardinī at Sergarh. All are in *rekhā* style. They are badly dilapidated and devoid of decoration except for the larger shrine on the south. But these are not built uniformly at the four corner of the main shrine as found usually in a *pañchāyatana* temple. All these subsidiary shrines contain Śiva-*liṅgam* inside the sanctum. It is a very interesting feature that in a Śakti temple the subsidiary shrines contain Śiva-*liṅgam*. It seems that Śakti worship dominated over Śiva worship or Śaivism in that region at that time.

The shrine towards the north measures 1.22 m square at the base. On vertical elevation it has four fold divisions like *piṣṭa, bāḍa, gaṇḍi* and *mastaka*. Probably, the *mastaka* portion is ruined in course of time. The height of the temple is about 2.51 m. The doorjambs are plain. The doorway measures 48 cm by 65 cm. The *mastaka* of the temple is consisted of a *beki*, and *āmalaka* and *kalaśa*. The presiding deity inside the sanctum is a Śiva-*liṅgam*.

The subsidiary shrine at the backside of tile main shrine is in *rekhā* order. It is square on plan and measures 75 cm at the base. On vertical elevation it is divided into three fold divisions like *piṣṭa, bāḍa* and *gaṇḍi*. Now *mastaka* is not existed. The *pābhāga* has three mouldings. The height of the temple is 2.13 m. There are two niches on the doorjambs on both sides for the placement of *pārśva-devatās*. Inside the sanctum a Śiva-*liṅgam* is installed along with *śakti paṭṭa*.

The subsidiary shrine towards the south side is in *rekhā* order. It measures 65 cm square at the base. On vertical elevation it has three fold divisions like *piṣṭa, bāḍa* and *gaṇḍi*. The *mastaka* is totally ruined. The height of the temple is 2.13 m. The doorway measures 39 cm by 85 cm. The doorjamb is ornately carved and made of chlorite. The jambs are carved with *vanalatā* scrollwork and *haṁsa* design. The *dvārapālas* are housed in niches similar to those of the *khākharā* shrine. They appear in mirror image poses with their body facing away from the door and their head turned back. The front leg is uplifted and placed on the blade of an axe, while their arms are crossed in relaxed pose. This is an unusual pose which suggests outside influence. The lintel is detached. A Gajalakṣmī is carved at the centre with Lakṣmī in a pose identical to the example of the other *khākharā* temples. A Śiva-*liṅgam* is installed inside the sanctum. The shrine is built of laterite stone.

The subsidiary shrine towards the south corner is facing towards east. On plan it is square of 1.22 m at the base. This shrine has no *mastaka*. The height of the temple is 3.65 m. There is a Śiva-*liṅgam* inside the sanctum. The doorjamb is decorated with three bands of scrollworks. But no Gajalakṣmī image is found on the lintel. The *rāhā-pagas* at the *bāḍa* portion have niches for *pārśva-devatās.*

There are large numbers of loose sculptures of various cultic affiliation kept in the temple complex. Which suggest the site and its surrounding as a flourishing centre of Buddhism, Jainism, Vaiṣṇavism, Śaivism, Śaktism and the Śaura cult during 9th-10th centuries. Some of these images are inserted into the niches of the Khajūreśvara Śiva temple, a newly constructed temple in the site. The images found here are like the river goddesses, three Sūrya images and two images of Mahiṣamardinī, one of Varāha, one image of Viṣṇu along with the images of Mahākāla, Gaṇeśa and Kārttikeya. Iconographically and stylistically, most of these images as well as the doorframes can be ascribed to the ninth century.

Nārāyaṇī Temple at Chilika

The temple of Nārāyaṇī (Plate 16) is situated in the village Bakuti near the township of Chilika about four km from the national highway leading to Rambha on the foot of Bhaleri mountain. It is situated in the tehsil of Khallikote and in the district of Ganjam. The temple is in *khākharā* order and built of monolithic stone. It is painted with barnish. It is facing towards the west. A ten-armed Mahiṣamardinī in the name of Nārāyaṇī is worshipped as the presiding deity of the temple. As stated by the priest the temple is built by the king of Khallikote, Harihara Mardaraj. A perennial stream is flowing in front of the temple. Originally, the temple has no *jagamohana.* But recently a structure is added to the temple.

Plan

On plan the exterior of the temple is square of 3.34 m at the base. There is a rectangular modern structure, which covers the temple upto *gaṇḍi* portion. Behind the temple there is a kitchen room for preparation of *bhōga* which is also a later addition.

Elevation

On vertical elevation the temple has three fold divisions like *bāḍa, gaṇḍi* and *mastaka.* The height of the temple is 4.56 m. It directly rises from the ground level.

Bāḍa

It has a *triaṅga bāḍa* having three fold divisions like *pābhāga, jāṅgha* and *baraṇḍa.* There are no mouldings in the *pābhāga* portion. The *jāṅgha* portion is also plain except the *pārśva-devatā* niches on the *rāhā-paga.* The niches are carved within the *vajra-muṇḍī* design. The niches have both *talagarbhikā* and *ūrdhvagarbhikā* design. The niches measure 61 cm by 30 cm in size. The *baraṇḍa* is consisted of a single moulding. Three female deities are placed inside the *pārśva-devatā* niches which are very crudely carved of sand stone along with the temple.

Gaṇḍi

The *bāḍa* portion is topped by the *gaṇḍi.* The *vajra-muṇḍī* design of the *bāḍa* is extended upto the lower portion of the *gaṇḍi* and above the *vajra-muṇḍī* a *rekhā-muṇḍī* is carved at the upper portion of the *gaṇḍi.* On the east and the west side two divine images are placed above the *rekhā-muṇḍī.*

Mastaka

The *khākharā-mastaka* of the temple is separated from the *gaṇḍi* by a recess (Plate 17). The centre of all the four sides is decorated with *vajra-mastaka* design. At the centre of the crest line of the *khākharā-mastaka* are placed the usual elements like *āmalaka, kalaśa, āyudha* and *dhvaja.* At the end of the *mastaka* two seating elephants are depicted facing towards the north and the south, which is a unique feature as in other cases lions are represented.

Sanctum

The sanctum is square on plan and dark inside. It measures 1.52 m at the base. The presiding deity, Nārāyaṇī is enshrined within the sanctum. She is flanked by Rudrāṇī in the left side and Brahmāṇī in the right side. All the three deities inside the sanctum are made out of the same stone with that of the temple.

Doorjamb

Now, the doorjambs are covered with marbal plates. But at the base of the doorjamb door guards are represented within the niches. The entrance of the sanctum measures 33 cm in width and 1.27 cm in height.

Presiding Deity

The presiding deity of the temple is goddess Nārāyaṇī. She is a ten-armed Mahiṣamardinī (Plate 18). She is made of sand stone with that of the temple. She measures 1.27 m by 60 cm in height. She is flanked by two goddesses like Rudrāṇī and Brahmāṇī. She holds *khaḍga, sara, triśūla, chakra, śūla* in right hands and *paraśu, śaṅkha, aṅkuśa, ḍhāla* and *sarpa* in her left hands. She is under active worship by the people of the locality.

Recently, a Śiva-*liṅgam* is worshipped in front of the temple. Towards the north of this temple at a distance of about 80 m there is a Bana-Durgā temple measuring 3.4 m in length, 4.64 m in wide and about 3.4 m in height. As the *khākharā* style was introduced during the Bhauma epoch this small shrine and its presiding deity may be dated back to the Bhauma period, i.e. ninth century CE.

Gaurī Temple at Bhubaneswar

The temple of Gaurī (Plate 19) is situated within the compound of Kedāreśvara at Bhubaneswar. This temple is in *khākharā* order and consisted of a *vimāna* and a *jagamohana*. As a *khākharā* temple it belongs to the Vaitāl *deula* group, but in respect of its decorative details it is more akin to the Mukteśvara Śiva temple of the *rekhā* order. The presiding deity of the temple is a beautiful life size image of Pārvatī. It is built of khondalite stone. The *mastaka* of the *vimāna* and *jagamohana* are newly constructed.

There is an interesting description in *Śiva Purāṇa* on the naming of Gaurī, Pārvatī, daughter of Himālaya was black in complexion, so she was affectionately called "Kālī" (black in colour) by Lord Śiva. But once some how Lord Śiva got irritated and addressed Pārvatī as Kālī which deeply pained her. She left her husband's abode and took shelter in a cave. Pārvatī took to severe penance in order to change her complexion. Brahmā was pleased in her prayer and granted boon of fair complexions. Since then Pārvatī is known as Gaurī.[25]

The Kumārariga plate of Bhauma-Kara queen records that Daṇḍī Mahādevī, who was a patron of Śaktism considered herself as the incarnation of Gaurī and built the Gaurī temple in the *Ekāmra Kṣetra*, K.C. Panigrahi, however, stylistically, assigns it to the second quarter of the tenth century CE.

In course of time the Gaurī temple has been partially mined as depicted in the book of M.M. Gangooly. The *mastaka* of the main temple and the *jagamohana* have undergone restoration. These reconstructions are bereft of decoration and plastered with whitewash which contrasts the purplish-red body of the original structure.[26] The temple is facing towards the east.

Plan

On plan the *vimāna* is rectangular and *pañcharatha* corresponding to the five offset projections on each side at the base while the *jagamohana* is square on plan. The *vimāna* measures 4.5 m by 3.34 m at the base.

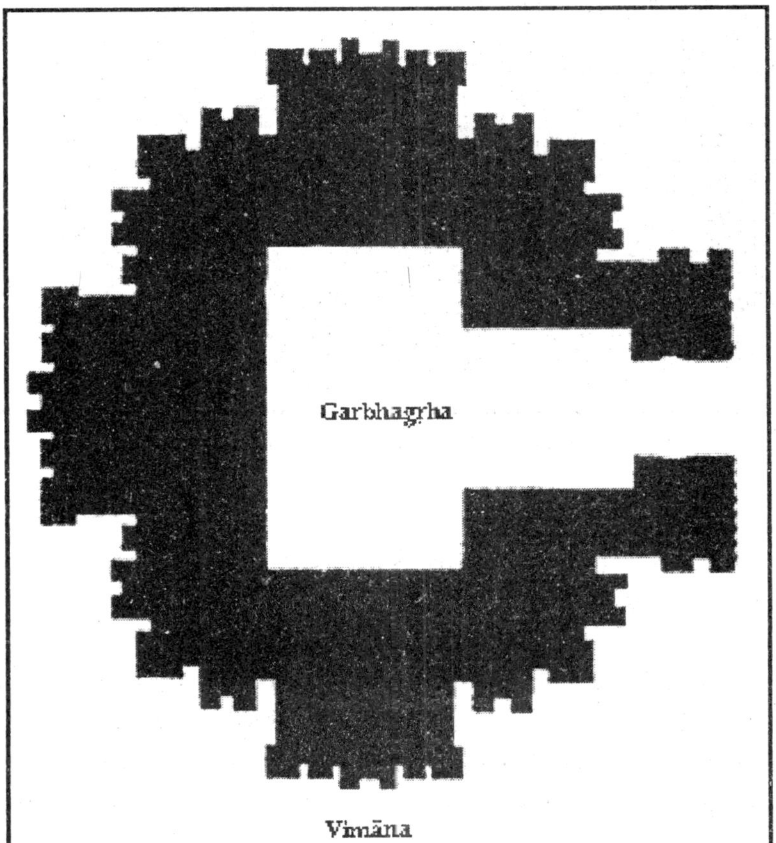

Fig. 8. Ground plan of Gaurī temple, Bhubaneswar

Elevation

On vertical elevation the temple has four divisions like *piṣṭa, bāḍa, gaṇḍi* and *mastaka.* The *vimāna* is not of great height. The *vimāna* rests on a very low platform of *tri-ratha* design. The lower part of it is decorated with *yakṣas* with uplifted hands, as if they are raising the entire temple structure. The *piṣṭa* measures 35 cm in height. The height of the temple is approximately 8 m.

Fig. 9. Elevation of *bāḍa* of Gaurī temple, Bhubaneswar

Bāḍa

The *bāḍa* has two fold divisions like *pābhāga* and *jāṅgha* from bottom to top. The height of the *bāḍa* is 2.50 m. It has five vertical segments or *paga* divisions which continue upto the *mastaka.* There is an improvement in the treatment of *bāḍa* of this temple than that of Vaitāl temple. The *pābhāga* is 68 cm in height and consisted of five mouldings on the *rāhā* and *anuratha paga,* but has four mouldings on the *kaṇikā paga.* There is a *talagarbhikā* below the *anuratha* niches, so that, this *paga* has a tripartite design. A *kiriṭa* design appears on the *khūra* moulding and all of the mouldings are richly decorated. The recesses of the *pābhāga* are decorated with *nartikās.*

The *kaṇikā paga,* of the *jāṅgha* portion is carved in scrollwork with overlying *alamba* motifs of a *kīrttimukha* dripping festoons of pearls from the mouth. The figure motifs are either a *mithuna* image or the *alasa-kanyās.* The *anuratha paga* is designed with *khākharā-muṇḍī* and contains subsidiary niches. This *paga* is crowned by a *kalaśa.* The central or *rāhā-pagas* project considerably from the body of the temple. It contains the *pārśva-devatā* niche flanked by pilasters. These pilasters are treated like that of *kaṇikā paga.* The images of *pārśva-devatā* are carved out of separate blocks of stone. The *nāga-nāgī stambha* appear on the recesses between the *rāhā* and *anuratha paga* on the longer west side. Here, we do not find the *baraṇḍi* division of the *bāḍa* portion.

Gaṇḍi

The *gaṇḍi* consists of two sections. Here the *kaṇikā pagas* are not divided into usual *bhūmi* divisions by *bhūmi-āmalās.* On the longer west side, the *gaṇḍi* has a *saptaratha* plan produced by the extension of the *nāga-nāgī stambhas* which creates an additional *paga.* The *bhūmi* divisions are decorated with *khākharā-muṇḍīs.* The designs of the lower *bhūmi* are aligned with the *pagas* of the *bāḍa* and continue their vertical thrust. The *kaṇikā* as well as the *anuratha pagas* are decorated in the manner of two super imposed *khākharā-muṇḍīs* crowned by *kalaśa.* The second *bhūmi* has a *niche* at its base. The *rāhā-pagas* are decorated with two superimposed *bho* motifs. The *bho* motif is consisted of a large *chaitya* with a projecting *kīrttimukha* at the top. The entire body of the temple except the *mastaka* looks purplish-red because of the application of paints.

The *viṣama* terminating the *gaṇḍi* consists of a bold *pheṇi* mouldings decorated with *padmaprasta* scrollwork. The *beki* recess is filled with perforated *jālī* designs.

Mastaka

The *mastaka*[27] of the temple had been ruined completely and its place is taken by a recently built structure. So, the *mastaka* has undergone restoration and as such it's plastered and white ashed surface presents a dire contrast to the lavishly decorated purplish-red body of the temple. As reconstructed now, resembling, an inverted bowl, it consists of two *khākharā* separated by a recess with a surmounting *kalaśa* and finial. The projecting *udyatā* lions, four crowing the lower *khākharā* and two on the top *khākharā* were added to the temple at the time of its last restoration.[28]

Jagamohana

The original *jagamohana* has been damaged. The present *jagamohana* is a modern structure. Probably the original *jagamohana* was a *pīḍha deula* like that of Mukteśvara temple[29], which is contemporary to this temple. This shows a developed stage in the evolution of *jagamohana* of *khākharā* temples. It is constructed in a new style which is not heavily plastered and white washed. The *jāṅgha* of the present structure is divided into two storeyes by a *bandhana* or stringcourse. The modern constructed roof has five *pīḍha* mouldings crowned by a *ghaṇṭā āmalaka* and *kalaśa* surmounted by a trident. The only sculptural decoration are the *beki Bhairavas* and *dopichchha* lion supporting the *ghaṇṭā* and *udyatā* lions projecting out above a platform at the level of the third *pīḍha.*

Presiding Deity

The presiding deity of the temple inside the sanctum is Gaurī, a form of goddess Pārvatī. She is standing in *samabhaṅga* pose. She is four-armed. Her lower hands are held in *abhaya-mudrā* and *varada-mudrā.* In her upper two hands she holds *kuṭhāra* and *pāśa.* The image is made of chlorite stone. She is beautifully decorated with different kinds of ornaments.

Cult Images

The niches of the Gaurī temple are empty, but some scattered sculptures within the compound form a part of decorative motifs. On the south wall of the compound an image of Kārttikeya is affixed which is badly eroded. Kārttikeya stands in slightly flexed pose holding the *śakti* in his uplifted front right hand while his back right hand is extended in *varada-mudrā.* Both of his left hands hold the rooster cock which is additionally supported by a small image of Devasenā standing on the lower left corner.

Decorative Motifs and Secular Images

The *alasa-kanyā* found in plenty, in the outer wall of Gaurī temple are remarkable for their charm and delicate modeling. They are depicted in various seductive poses. They stand on louts cushion and also lotus creeper forms a canopy over their heads. An image of an *alasa-kanyā* holding a mirror close to her face appears as space filler flanking the top of the *khākharā-muṇḍī* of the lower *bhūmi*. There is a motif in which a monkey is togged at the garments of a woman clinging to tree branch.

In Gaurī temple *mithuna* images are carved in high relief in the north and the west corner of the *deula* in contrast to the *mithuna* images of the Vaitāl *deula* carved on the *jāṅgha*. The *mithuna* partners of Gaurī temple are more active and intertwined like creepers. The other smaller *mithuna* images appear in the niches at the base of *khākharā-muṇḍī* of the second *bhūmi* of the *gaṇḍi*, There are also *mithuna* scenes, though diminutive in scale, on the sloping roof of the eave covering the *pārśva-devatā* niche. There are also two displayed female figures with legs widespread, appearing in the lower *vajra-mastaka* on the western face of the *gaṇḍi*. In this temple in the western side of the *gaṇḍi* in *anuratha* recess there appears a well-preserved face or a *nāgī* coiled around the *stambha*. There is also motif of dwarf *bhāra-rakṣakas* on the outer facade of the *piṣṭa*. At the top of the *kaṇikā pagas* the *kīrttimukhas* are depicted. It is also depicted at the apex of *vajra-mastaka* design. The atlantid carved in shallow niches on the square capitals of the pilasters, of the *kaṇikā* and *rāhā* are look pot-like. There is also a *nandika-mukha* on the *khūra*-moulding of the *pābhāga*. There are also diminutive standing female figures in *chaitya* designs on the same moulding or in the vertical bars connecting the two top mouldings. In addition to the double *gajakrāntas* on the pillars there are also *jāgratas* separated by a *kalaśa* at the top of the *muṇḍī* design. There is a big *makara* motif as gargoyle on the *piṣṭa* in front of the *rāhā* on the north side and also many diminutive *makara* motifs appear at the ends of scrollwork on horizontal mouldings. There are many small animals like deer, carved on the sloping upper surface of the *baraṇḍis* of the *gaṇḍi*.

Other popular motifs depicted on this temple are scrollworks like *vanalatā* and *ratikera*, foliage *ālamba* design near the top of pilasters, horizontal moulding of the *vimānika, khākharā-muṇḍī, bho* type *vajra-mastaka,* etc.

Like Mukteśvara temple it is also profusely ornamented. So, it must have been built around the same date as the Mukteśvara. On stylistical[30] ground this temple can be assigned to tenth century CE.

Vārāhī Temple at Chaurasi

One of the most beautiful Śākta temples of Orissa, Vārāhī *deula* (Plate 20) is situated in the village Chaurasi on the bank of the river Prāchī, about 2 km from Amareśvara and about 14 km from Gop on the road to Kakatpur in Puri district. The temple is in *khākharā* order and dedicated to Vārāhī, one of the *mātṛkās*. As suggested by Debala Mitra, it is the only surviving temple among seven erected in the region dedicated to the *Sapta Mātṛkās*.[31] Prāchī Valley has been the major religious site of Orissa from eighth to thirteenth centuries CE having remains of Jaina, Buddhist and Hindu monuments.[32] Particularly, *śākta* and *tantric* cults appear to be more popular in the area, as evident from the remains of *śākta* and *tantric* monuments. Among the popular goddesses worshipped were Mahiṣamardinī, Maṅgalā, Chāmuṇḍā, Vārāhī, etc. The *Śilpa Prakāśa*, a medieval Orissan *tantric* text on temple architecture, found at Nimapada and another text of this kind also found near Kakatapur in this area testify to the importance of the *Kaulāchāra* sect.[33]

The temple of Vārāhī is consisted of a rectangular *khākharā* type *vimāna* and an oblong *jagamohana* with roof made up of two sloping terraces. It seems it is one of the earliest temples in eastern Orissa to incorporate the new architectural features, filtering into Orissa from central India via the Mahānadī Valley, although the temple is small in stature yet it is lavishly decorated with finely carved motifs. Stylistically, the temple may be assigned to the first part of tenth century CE. The temple is built of sandstone locally known as *kuṇḍa paṭhāra* or also known as *naraja paṭhāra* after the quarry at Naraj about 50 km from Chaurasi. The temple is facing towards the east.

Plan

Both the *vimāna* and the *jagamohana* are rectangular on plan and stand on same axial plane. The *vimāna* has five offset projections at the base. The *vimāna* measures approximately 5.44 m by 3.80 m at the base and the *jagamohana* measures 9.42 m by 7 m at the base. There are nine offset projections on longer side of the *jagamohana* at the base.

Elevation

The *vimāna* has four sections on its vertical alignment, viz. *piṣṭa, bāḍa, gaṇḍi*

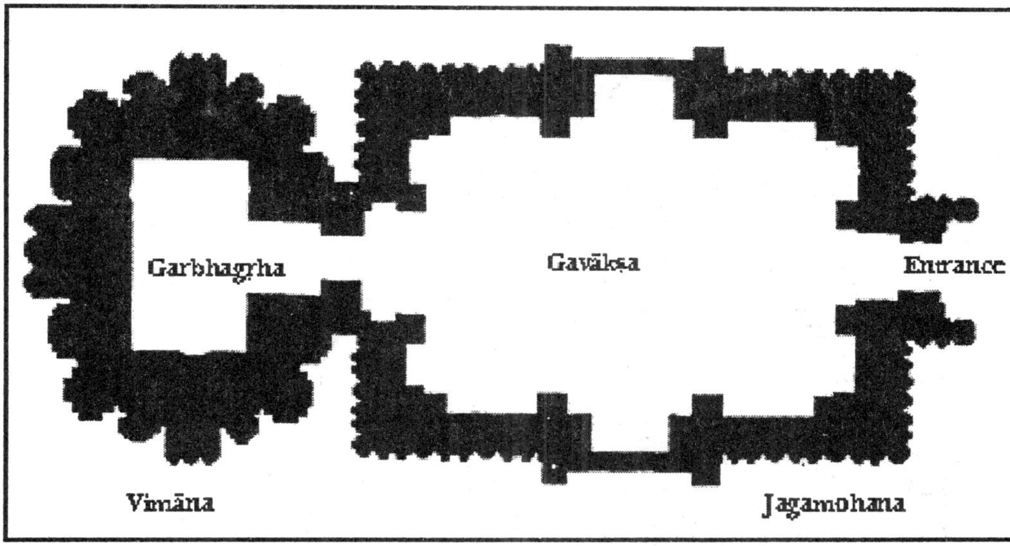

Fig. 10. Ground plan of Vārāhī temple, Chaurasi

and *mastaka*. The *vimāna* measures 7.60 m in height. The *jagamohana* has also same divisions like *piṣṭa*, *bāḍa*, flat roofed *gaṇḍi* and a *kalaśa* at the top. Both *vimāna* and *jagamohana* are resting on same platform or *piṣṭa* of 70 cm in height, which has no decorations.

Bāḍa

The *bāḍa* has three fold divisions like *pābhāga*, *jāṅgha* and *baraṇḍa*. The *pābhāga* is 81 cm high and consisted of three mouldings like *khūra*, *kumbha* and *paṭṭa*. These are decorated with creepers and scrollwork. The *rathas* of *pagas* are clearly divided into five vertical facets. The *rāhā-paga* on the south and north sides are designed as *khākharā-muṇḍī* with its niche resting on the *pābhāga*. The upper portion of the niche is designed as an *ūrdhvagarbhikā*. This *ūrdhvagarbhikā* is also designed like *khākharā-muṇḍī*. A thin *talagarbhikā* appears below the niche. The niche is framed on each side by a pilaster relieved with scrollwork. The *rāhā-paga* on the longer side is the broadest one and its upper portion filled in with an *ūrdhvagarbhikā* contains three *khākharā-muṇḍīs*. A band of decorative scrollwork frames the inside of the niche, relieved with a *dvāra lalāṭabimba* panel above. The recesses between *pagas* are filled

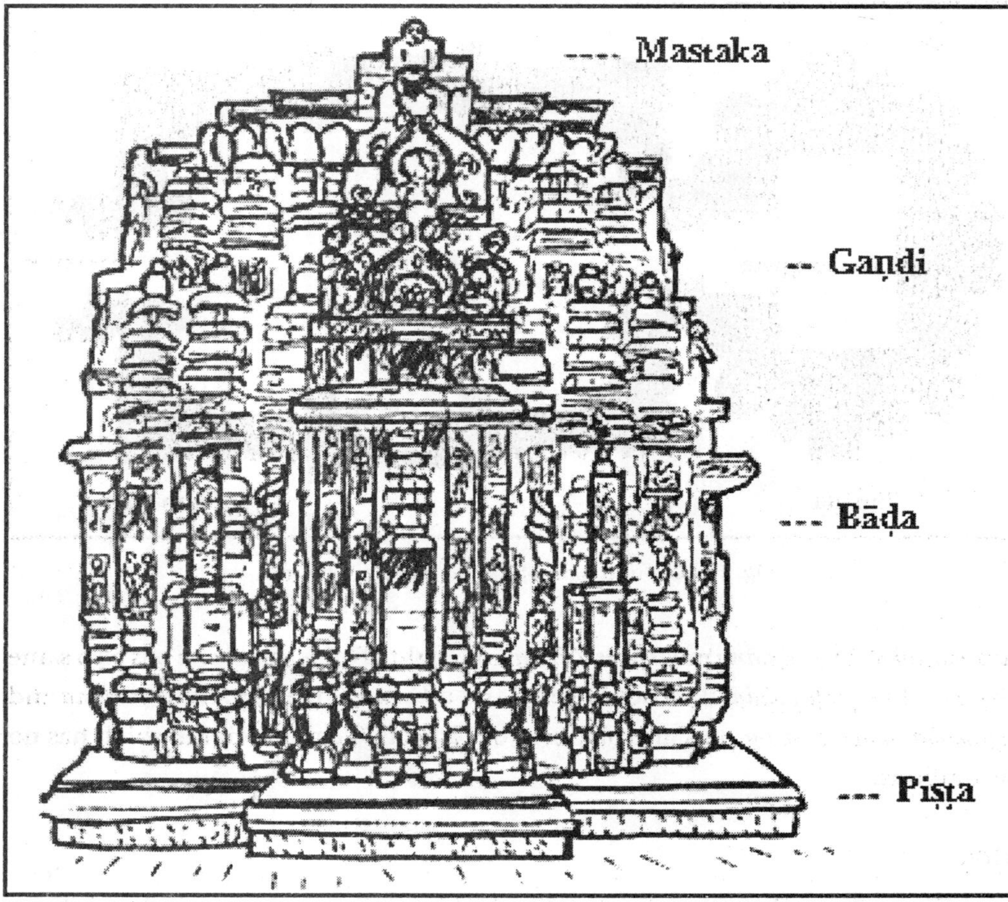

Fig. 11. Elevation of Vārāhī temple, Chaurasi

up with the entwined *nāga* and *nāgī* carrying garlands and offerings. This is the first example of this motif appearing in the *anuratha* recess.

The *kaṇikā paga* on all sides of the *vimāna* consists of a central vertical facet relieved with beautiful scrollwork above a *tala-bandhanā*. The upper portion of the *paga* has a shallow niche filled in with *mithuna* motif. There is an *ūrdhva-bandhanā* above the niche. The *anuratha-paga* on the north and south sides are multifaceted, but narrower and lack the niche design. The *anuratha-paga* on the lower south side is similar and in the base of the *nāga stambha* a *gaja-krānta* motif is depicted. These *stambhas* begin above the *pābhāga*.

Gaṇḍi

The *ūrdhva-bandhanā* above the niches turns into an ineffective *baraṇḍa*. Here *baraṇḍa* acts as the first *bhūmi* of the *gaṇḍi* or as the crowning member or the *bāḍa*. It is designed like a row of *khākharā-muṇḍīs* aligned with the *pagas* of tile *bāḍa* and decorated with a small *vajra-mastaka* on its top mouldings. On the *kaṇikā* and *amuratha pagas* these *muṇḍīs* are crowned by *kalaśa* on the north and south sides. But on the lower side only *kaṇikā paga* is there in this design. The *rāhā-pagas* in this portion are designed as niches for *pārśva-devatās*. The recesses between *amuratha* and *kaṇikā* are relieved with *śālabhañjikās* above the *nāga-stambhas*, while the recesses separating the *rāhā* from the *anuratha* are decorated with amorous couples. The second *bhūmi* division is also designed like the first *bhūmi-baraṇḍa*. But here there is a recess at the base which is decorated with niches on the *anuratha* and *kaṇikā* on the west, north and south sides. The niches contain the figures of *mithunas* while the recess contains the figure of *śālabhañjikā*. The *anuratha paga* on the shorter side is designed as *vajra-mastaka* and the *rāhā* is as *tri-ratha*. The *rāhā-paga* of this portion consists of a large *chaitya* medallion formed by strings of pearls dripping from a small *kīrttimukha* mask projecting at its apex. The lower *khākharā-muṇḍī* of the *rāhā* contains an image of two-armed Vārāhī in *lalitāsana* holding a skull-cup in the left hand and a fish in the right. The recesses between the *khākharā-muṇḍī* are decorated with *chaitya* window motifs, animal frieze, etc. On the longer sides of the medallion (front and back), a dwarf *yakṣya* with one leg uplifted and held a club in one hand placing the other hand on chick is depicted. For the first time the *bho* type *vajra-mastaka* appears on the *gaṇḍi* of the temple. On the north and south sides the *kīrttimukha* motif is replaced by large *udyatā* lion. Thus, many new motifs appearing for the first time in this temple become a standard decoration in the later temple. Now, the backside *rāhā* niche is filled in by a Sūrya image, while the south niche by a Gaṇeśa image, but the north niche is vacant.

Mastaka

The *mastaka* (Plate 21) is a *khūra*-shaped *khākharā* designed as *tri-ratha*. A *srahi* (splayed out moulding) decorated with lotus petals demarcated the *gaṇḍi* from the *mastaka*. The entire central projection is decorated with a *chaitya*-window having a *khākharā-muṇḍī* and a lion is depicted at the apex. The central crest running along the central axis has a *kalaśa* at the centre and *udyatā* lions at both the end.

Sanctum

The interior of the sanctum measures 3.42 m by 1.90 m. The roof consisting of a series of flat stones is supported by iron beams which rest on four inverted *khūra*-shaped corbels. A corbelled niche is found at the top, which lessens the load over the ceiling. There is *siṁhāsana* inside the sanctum on which the presiding deity is installed. The size of the throne is 1.93 m in width, 2.94 m in height and 1.15 m in length.

Doorjamb

The doorjamb of the sanctum is well decorated with pot-bellied *dvārapālikās* (female door keeper) one on each side and with different motifs like fan-shaped leave, fruits and scrollwork. The central band is decorated with a creeper flanked by frolicking boys playing on musical instruments in dancing pose. The *dvārapālikās* are depicted as pot-bellied figure holding skull-up and *pāśa* in their hands. The central portion of the lintel contains figure of Gajalakṣmī flanked by a couple of flying Gandharvas.

Jagamohana

The *jagamohana* of Vārāhī temple has *triaṅga bāḍa.* The lowest portion of the *jagamohana,* the *pābhāga* is consisted of a *khūra* and a *kumbha* decorated with *champaka* leaf and a third moulding designed as a *pīḍha* is decorated with small *chaityas* and an inverted *khūra* carved with creepers and scrollwork. It measures 66 cm in height. The *jāṅgha* is a single storeyed design decorated with *khākharā-muṇḍī* designs alternating with pilasters, three on each side of the *jālī* windows of its south and north walls. It measures 1.21 m in height. There is no *talagarbhikā* below the *muṇḍī* niche which consists of a single *bhūmi* capped by a splayed *pheṇi* surmounted by a *vajra-mastaka.* The *vajra-mastaka* is flanked by *bhāra-rakṣakas* and topped by a *kīrttimukha* while the thin pilasters alternating with the *muṇḍīs* are decorated with scrollwork above a *pūrṇa-ghaṭa* placed at the bottom. It is crowned by the dwarf atlantes at the top. But the corner pilasters are wider and crowned by *mithuna* figures. The base of these pilasters has *talabandhanā* design.

These pilasters are extending through the *pābhāga* mouldings unlike the *deula* where it begins above the *pābhāga.* The perforated *jālī* windows on the south and the north walls are ornately carved with creepers and scrollwork and are framed at the sides by *nāga-stambha.* A *khākharā-muṇḍī* is added on each side of the window containing a four-armed female guard. There are four insets, one at the centre of each side. The top inset is carved with figure of Gajalakṣmī, The bottom insets have each a seated figure in *rājalilāsana* posture. The side inset is filled in with *vidyādharas.* Above the window there is tall *vajra-muṇḍī* design. On the front east side of the *jagamohana* there are only three pilasters on each side of the entrance portal. The *khākharā-muṇḍī* of the *jāṅgha* portion is filled in with images like *dikpālas, dikpālikās,* Gaṇeśa, Gaṅgā and Yamunā.

The *baraṇḍa* at the top of the *bāḍa* consists of projecting *pīḍha* moulding with surmounting recess. It is 41 cm in height. This moulding is decorated with scrollwork while its sloping upper face contains miniature dancing figures and animal motifs.

The roof consists of *pīḍhas* in two tiers. The recess separating the two tiers is decorated with shallow niches alternating with *pūrṇa-ghaṭas.* The niches contain erotic figures. The cornices below the two projecting ones are decorated with scenes from the *Rāmāyaṇa* hunting scenes and scene of animal processions. The flat roof is crowned by a monolithic *kalaśa* placed on a square pedestal.

The interior of the *jagamohana* is plain. There are twelve engaged pilasters, four on each walls of the north and south side and two are there, flanking the entrance portal on the east and west.

The doorframe of the *jagamohana* is similar in style to that of the sanctum. It is framed by a *nāga-nāgī stambha,* at the right and the other on the left side. The projecting architrave above the lintel is relieved with *navagrahas.* The doorframe consists of three mouldings decorated with the *kuṭilā, gelaba* and *jalapatra* scroll motif. Though the Gajalakṣmī panel of the lintel is partly covered with multiple coats of whitewash yet an image of Lakṣmī in seated posture may be seen. The niches at the base of the doorjambs are filled in with *dvārapālikās* (four-armed female guards), The base of the outside jambs adjacent to the *dvārapāla* is carved with a *nāga* on the proper right side holding a garland and a *nāgī* on the left holding a vase in front of her body with both hands. Both these figures have serpent hood over their head.

The *yūpa* in front of the *jagamohana* indicates the *tāntric* nature of the temple.

Cult Images

Two of the *pārśva-devatās* are in situ, Sūrya on the west side and Gaṇeśa on the south side of the temple while the niche on the north side is empty. According to the *kaula* doctrine, Vārāhī represents the *jñāna*—aspect of the *śakti* as such; it should have contained an image of Bhairava, the male counterpart of the *jñānaśakti*.[34] Hence, it is difficult to ascertain how Sun is associated as the *pārśva-devatā* in a *śākta-tāntric* temple. Most probably the original image of this niche (*śākta* character) was lost and the image from some other shrine was fixed here later on. The image of the pot-bellied Gaṇeśa (52 cm by 30 cm) is four-armed and in standing posture. He holds in his lower left hand a hatchet, upper left a bowl of *laḍḍūs* (sweet), in upper right a broken tusk and in lower right a rosary. His mount (mouse) is depicted at the base of the pedestal. He is wearing beautiful ornaments like, anklets, *sarpa-upavīta*, and necklace, a tiara with *kiriṭamukuṭa*, snake-armlet, and finger rings.

The image of Sūrya is two-armed and it is finely carved in chlorite stone. He is seated in *padmāsana* on his chariot which is drawn by seven horses. He holds the stalk of a full-blown lotus in each hand. He is decorated with beautiful ornaments. His hair is arranged in tall *mukuṭa* (crown). The charioteer Aruṇa is shown down to the waist. The images of Daṇḍī and Piṅgala appear at the corners of the chariot.

The niches of the corner *muṇḍī* contain *dikpālas* and the second *muṇḍīs* contain their *śakti* (*dikpālikās*) while the niches of the third *muṇḍī* on the longer sides of the north and the south contain Śaivite deities such as Gaṇeśa, Kārttikeya and a four-armed Durgā. The niches on either side of the *jālī* window house four-armed *mahāvidyās* or *āvaraṇa-śaktis*.[35] The images of river goddesses Gaṅgā and Yamunā housed in the niches on the north and the south flanks of the entrance projection. Four guard images are depicted on the *gavākṣa*. Inside the *jagamohana* are two detached images of pot-bellied Vārāhī in *ardhaparyaṅka* posture. One has two arms and the other has four arms. At the top of the oval halo of the images are carved *vidyādharas*.

Secular Images and Decorative Motifs

Being a *śākta-tāntric* temple many scenes of *tāntric* natures are depicted on walls of the temple. Besides these ritualistic scenes, numerous *mithuna* images are depicted on the *gaṇḍi* and in the recess separating the *pīḍhas* of the roof of *jagamohana*. There are also *bhikṣāṭanamūrti, bhāra-rakṣaka* figures, scenes from *Rāmāyaṇa* animal figures, *nāyikās*, hunting scenes, etc. depicted on the outer walls of both *vimāna* and *jagamohana*. Other important decorative motifs are *kīrttimukha, vajra-mastaka, udyatā* lion, etc. The scrollwork appears on the doorframe and *vanalatā* motifs appear on the *pagas* and pilasters. The motifs are subtly carved and at varied to make the temple most beautiful one.

Presiding Deity

The presiding deity of the temple Vārāhī (1.85 m and 83 cm) is carved in chlorite (Plate 22). There are two cut marks on her shoulder and belly; otherwise it is in perfect state of preservation. She is seated in *lalitāsana* on a cushion; her right foot is resting on her buffalo mount carved on the pedestal. She is two-armed holding a fish in the right hand and a skull-up in the left one. She is decorated with various ornaments such as anklets, armlets, finger-rings, necklace, earring, etc. There is a *tiara* on her forehead. She is a goddess of terrific look with three eyes, boar face and pot belly. She has curly-hair. Stylistically, the temple can be assigned to tenth century CE.

Akhadachaṇḍī Temple of Bhubaneswar

Akhadachaṇḍī temple (Plate 23) is a small Śākta temple dedicated to the Mahiṣāsuramardinī Durgā. This temple is situated in the south-western embankment of Bindusagar tank at Badu Sahi in the old town of Bhubaneswar. It is 15 m east of Mārkaṇḍeśvara temple and to the north-west of Mohinī temple at a distance of 30 m. The temple is facing towards south and the presiding deity is facing towards east. Various religious sacraments like Durgāṣṭamī and Bālabhoga are performed here. The temple is maintained by Bhubaneswar Municipal Corporation. It is in fair state of preservation. The temple was repaired by the Odisha State Archaeology under the X and XI Finance Commission Award. The temple is surrounded by Bindusagar tank in the east at a distance of 6.40 m, Mārkaṇḍeya temple in the west and private residential buildings in the southern side.

Architectural Features

The temple is constructed in the Kaliṅgan style using coarse-grained sandstone. The main temple is a *khākharā deula.* It is rectangular on plan measuring 1.28 m x 1.83 m. On elevation, the *vimāna* is of *khākharā* order measuring 42.94 m in height from *pābhāga* to *mastaka.* From bottom to the top the temple has *bāḍa, gaṇḍi* and *mastaka.* With fivefold division the *bāḍa* measures 1.74 m. At the bottom the *pābhāga* measures 0.26 m in height. *Jāṅgha* measuring 0.52 m is segmented into *tala jāṅgha* and *upara jāṅgha* by a set of *bandhana* moulding. *Bandhana* measures 0.08 m and *baraṇḍa* measures in 0.26 m. *Gaṇḍi* of the temple is in *khākharā* order which is arranged in three tires with a semi cylindrical roof. The *mastaka* of the temple consists of a *kalaśa* flanked by two *gajakrānta* on either side.

Decorative Features

The doorjamb is decorated with two plaster design measuring 1.10 m x 0.65 m. Besides the main entrance there are two subsidiary gateways in the eastern and northern walls. These two gateways are uniform in measurement measuring 0.92 m x 0.59 m. Akhadachaṇḍī temple whose presiding deity is Mahiṣāsuramardinī Durgā (Plate 24) is assigned to the tenth century CE.

Khākharā Temple Inside Mukteśvara Temple Compound at Bhubaneswar

There is a small *khākharā* order of temple inside the compound of Mukteśvara temple at Bhubaneswar (Plate 25). The temple is in *tri-ratha* design and is facing towards the east. It is made of sandstone. At present the presiding deity of the temple is a Śiva-*liṅgam* with *śakti paṭṭa.*

Plan

The temple is rectangular and *tri-ratha* on plan and measures 1.75 by 1.55 at the base.

Elevation

On vertical elevation it has four fold divisions like *piṣṭa, bāḍa, gaṇḍi* and *mastaka.* The height of the temple is 3 m. It stands on a very high platform.

Bāḍa

It has a *triaṅga bāḍa* or three fold divisions like *pābhāga, jāṅgha* and *baraṇḍa.* The height of the *bāḍa* is 1.55 m. It has no *pābhāga* mouldings. It is 34 cm high. The *jāṅgha* has single storeyed design. It has only *rāhā-paga* at the center of the *bāḍa.* The *rāhā-pagas* have *pārśva-devatā* niches. The niches are carved within *pīḍha-muṇḍī* design. It has five mouldings. The *jāṅgha* measures 50 cm high. The *pārśva-devatās* found in all three niches are Pārvatī, Gaṇeśa and Kārttikeya. The niches measure 32 cm by 33 cm. The *baraṇḍa* of the *bāḍa* has two mouldings.

Gaṇḍi

The *gaṇḍi* is almost plain and only the *pīḍha-muṇḍī* of the *bāḍa* is extended up to the *gaṇḍī* portion. But, on the front side above the sanctum doorway the *muṇḍī* design is extended up to the *mastaka* portion.

Mastaka

The *khākharā-mastaka* of the temple is separated from the *gaṇḍī* by a recess or *beki.* The *mastaka* is plain. At the top of the *mastaka* a *kalaśa* is placed.

Sanctum

The interior of the sanctum measures 1.10 by 70 cm. The height of sanctum is 1.70 cm. A Śiva-*liṅgam* with *śakti paṭṭa* is enshrined as presiding deity of the temple. But there is a niche of 75 by 115 on the backside wall of the sanctum. Probably originally, there was a Śākta deity inside the sanctum, as almost all *khākharā* temples in Orissa are meant for Śākta goddesses.

Doorjamb

The doorjambs are plain. But, the *dvārapālas* are carved at the base of the doorjambs and the *navagrahas* are depicted on the architrave.

Cult Images

On the north sidewall goddess Pārvatī is placed inside the niche. She is seating in *lalitāsana.* She is four-armed. She is seated on a prostrate corpse. Her lower right hand is in *abhaya-mudrā,* while her lower left hand is holding a *kalaśa.* The attribute of her upper right is indistinct, while she is holding a goad in her upper left hand. She is decorated with ornaments and wearing a sacred thread. Inside the western *pārśva-devatā* niche Kārttikeya is placed. He is two-armed. He is holding a goad in his right hand and a cock in his left hand. He is also seating in *lalitāsana* on a lotus cushion. He is wearing a sacred thread. He is wearing a *jaṭāmukūṭa.*

In the southern *pārśva-devatā* niche, Gaṇeśa is placed. He is seating in *lalitāsana.* He is holding a *laduka* in one of his left hands. In another left had he is holding an *aṅkuśa.* His right hands are holding a *kuṭhāra* and a goad.

Presiding Deity

At present the presiding deity of the temple is a Śiva-*liṅgam* with *śakti.* But the niche on the backside wall of the sanctum justify that the original deity might have been a Śākta goddess.

Stylistically, the temple can be assigned to the tenth century CE. This may be an exceptional case where a Śiva-*liṅgam* is enshrined in a *khākharā* order of temple because in Orissa only female deities are enshrined in this type of temple.

Uttarāyaṇī Ṭhakurānī Temple at Ghasiaundhati

The temple of goddess Uttarāyaṇī Ṭhakurānī is situated at Ghasiaundhati in the district of Puri at a distance of about 25 km from Bhubaneswar on the Nimapada road about 3 km from Narda chowque. She is locally known as Uttarāyaṇī Ṭhakurānī or Uparānī Buddhi. It is a very small *khākharā* temple. Architecturally, this temple has close similarity with the small *khākharā* temple inside the Mukteśvara temple compound. The temple was in dilapidated condition, which was recently renovated by the Department of State Archaeology. The temple is built of sand stone and is facing towards the east.

Plan

The *vimāna* is rectangular on plan, with one offset projection at the centre on each side. It is 3.37 m by 3.95 m at the base. But the platform is rectangular on plan and measures 5.4 m by 3.95 m at the base. The temple is *tri-ratha* on plan.

Elevation

The temple is constructed over a lofty platform of 1.62 m high, which is approached by a flight of steps. On elevation there are four fold divisions of the temple like *piṣṭa, bāḍa, gaṇḍi* and *mastaka.* The height of the *vimāna* is approximately 5.77 m. The platform is consisted of five courses of stone.

Bāḍa

The *bāḍa* of the temple is a *triaṅga bāḍa* or has threefold division like *pābhāga, jāṅgha* and *baraṇḍa.* There are four simple horizontal mouldings in the *pābhāga.* Its height is 53 cm. The *jāṅgha* of the *bāḍa* has single storeyed design. The central or *rāhā-paga* of the *bāḍa* is designed like a *rekhā-muṇḍī* where the niches for the *pārśva-devatās* are carved. This *rekhā-muṇḍī* is elongated up to the end of the *gaṇḍi* portion. Each niche measures 61 cm by 38 cm while the outer portion of the niche measures 1.33 m by 73 cm. All these niches are empty. Now, religious books are placed inside the niches by the local people. Above the niche there are projecting eaves. There is a recessed *kānthi* at the top of the *bāḍa.* On both sides of this *kānthi* recess there is a single projecting moulding.

Gaṇḍi

The *gaṇḍi* is devoid of decorations except a projecting lion on the front side above the doorway lintel of the sanctum. The *rekhā-muṇḍī* of the *bāḍa* is continued on the vertical thrust of *gaṇḍi* at the *rāhā-paga.* At the top of the *gaṇḍi* there are four simple horizontal mouldings.

Mastaka

The *khākharā-mastaka* of the *vimāna* has two divisions. At the top of the *mastaka* a *kalaśa* is installed. This *kalaśa* is tied with *nāga* images along with *ghaṇṭis* (bells) on four sides. This is known as *nāgabandha kalaśa.*

Sanctum

The sanctum is rectangular on plan. It measures 1.39 m wide and 3.52 m in length. The height of the ceiling from the floor of sanctum is 2.30 m. At the backside wall of the sanctum the pedestal of the *Devī* is carved with two mouldings. It is 1.26 m in height and 83 cm in width. Some other broken sculptures are kept inside the sanctum.

Doorjamb

There is no carving on the doorjambs. A small Iron Gate is fixed at the doorjamb, which is a recent addition.

Presiding Deity

The most fascinating feature of this temple is its graceful presiding deity. It is an image of a serpent deity. This is a rare specimen of sculptural art of Orissa. The upper part from the waist of the *Devī* is in human form (female) while the lower portion is serpent coil. The image is finely carved of chlorite stone. There is the canopy of a five-hooded snake over the head of the *Devī*. The image is well decorated with beautiful ornaments. The height of the image is 1.22 m.

The goddess is now in active worship by the local people. She is specially worshipped in each *saṁkrānti* day. She is offered burnt fish on *mahāṣṭamī* day, which is the most important festival of this temple. On the basis of its architectural features this temple can be assigned to tenth century CE.

Liyahari Temple at Ranipur-Jharial

Ranipur-Jharial in the Titilagarh sub-division of Bolangir district is one of the important religious centers in western Orissa. It was a flourishing *tīrtha* from the eighth to ninth centuries as evident by the numerous temples and ruins. This place is more popular as the centre of sixty-four *yoginīs* cult as evident from the existence of the circular sixty-four *yoginīs* temple. Besides this temple two other *khākharā* temples also exist here. Of the two *khākharā* temples, the one placed at the top of the outcrop and adjacent to the *chausatha-yoginīs pīṭha* is smaller than the other one. The second *khākharā* temple which is larger locally known as Liyahari *mandira* (Plate 26). It situated on the south-west side of the outcrop and near the Someśvara Śiva temple. The temple is facing towards the east.

Plan

The temple is rectangular and *tri-ratha* on plan. The temple is approximately 6.28 m by 5.28 m at the base. There is no *jagamohana* in front of this temple.

Elevation

This temple rises to a height of about 6.69 m. On vertical elevation it has four divisions like *piṣṭa, bāḍa, gaṇḍi* and *mastaka*. It is situated on a very low *piṣṭa*.

Bāḍa

On elevation the *bāḍa* has three fold divisions from bottom to top like *pābhāga, jāṅgha* and *baraṇḍa,* while there are three vertical offset projections on the *bāḍa*. The *jāṅgha* portion of this temple is devoid of decoration and only plain projection is seen at the centre of each side. The *baraṇḍa* is consisted of three plain mouldings. The central projection of the *baraṇḍa* at the sides and back is crowned by *chaitya* design that extends up to the *gaṇḍi* of the temple.

Gaṇḍi

The *gaṇḍi* has no *ratha* projections. It is designed as a large *chaitya* but traces of its central medallion are barely visible. On the front side above the sanctum doorway there is a large *chaitya* design with trace of its central medallion fairly visible.

Mastaka

The crowning *khākharā* member is separated from the *gaṇḍi* by a thin recess. The *chaitya* motif appears on the front and the back of the *khākharā* member. There is a *kalaśa* at the centre of the crest of the barrel-vaulted roof.

Sanctum

At present no image is found inside the sanctum. Inside the sanctum twelve engaged pilaster are used. But three other pilasters are constructed for the conservation of the temple later on.

Doorjamb

The entrance portal is very wide and has three opening with two pilasters and two pillars. The doorframe is fixed at the central opening. There is close similarity of this temple with the Nava-Durgā temple at Jogeśvara (Almora district in U.P.). This portal is crowned by a large projecting eave that is aligned with the *baraṇḍa.*

Probably, this temple was built to enshrine *Sapta Mātṛkās* or Mahiṣamardinī, because it seems that the artist had tried to carve out one image of Mahiṣamardinī on an escarpment of rock and two sets of *Sapta Mātṛkās* one on a boulder and the other on an escarpment of rock near this shrine. The temple is not under worship. This temple can be assigned to tenth century CE, contemporary to the date of the sixty-four *yoginīs* temple at the site.

Smaller *Khākharā* Temple at Ranjpur-Jharial

A very small *khākharā* order of temple (Plate 26) is standing in front of the sixty-four *yoginī* temple at Ranipur-Jharial. The temple is built of sandstone. It is facing towards the north. According to local tradition the temple was meant for the meditation of a *saint* as like most of the smaller temples of the site.

Plan

The temple is consisted of a *vimāna* only. It is *ekaratha* on plan. It measures 1.90 m in width and 2.28 m in length at the base. The *piṣṭa* of the temple measures 2.53 m by 2.13 m at the base.

Elevation

On vertical elevation the temple has four fold divisions like *piṣṭa, bāḍa, gaṇḍi* and *mastaka.* The height of the temple is 3.14 m. It stands on a low *piṣṭa* of 45 cm in height.

Bāḍa

It has a *triaṅga bāḍa.* The height of the *bāḍa* is 1.41 m. The three divisions of the *bāḍa* are *pābhāga, jāṅgha* and *baraṇḍa.* The *pābhāga* has two simple mouldings. It measures 48 cm in height. The niches are conspicuous by their absence of the *jāṅgha* portion. There is only the *rāhā* projection on the *bāḍa* of the temple. The *baraṇḍa* of the *bāḍa* is consisted of two mouldings.

Gaṇḍi

The *vajra-mastaka* designs are carved on all the four sides in a very crude way. On the front side of the The *gaṇḍi* of the temple is consisted of single *bhūmi* division, *gaṇḍi* above the *vajra-mastaka* design there is a projected rampant lion, which is in broken condition.

Mastaka

The *mastaka* of the shrine is separated from the *gaṇḍi* by a thin recess. It is a plain barrel vaulted roof. At present there is no *āmalaka* or *kalaśa* at the top of the roof.

Sanctum

The sanctum of the temple is rectangular on plan. It measures 1.39 cm by 81 cm at the base. The height of the ceiling is 1.90 m. There is no image or pedestal for the presiding deity inside the sanctum.

Doorjamb

This doorjamb is totally plain. It is consisted of two bands. The image of Gajalakṣmī is not depicted on the door lintel. The door way measures 1.9 m by 53 cm.

The temple can be assigned to tenth century CE as contemporaneous to the construction of the most of the temples of the site including sixty-four *yoginī* temple.

Pasachaṇḍī Temple at Badasahi

The village Badasahi is located at a distance of 25 km from Baripada. The Pasachaṇḍī temple is situated in the midst of the archaeological ruins of low mounds, large tanks, and loose sculptures of gods and goddesses of great antiquity.

But at present, nothing except a few laterites dressed stone slabs and the image of Nṛsiṁhī are found at the place. Being the personal property of the kings of

Baripada, the image of a Pasachaṇḍī was removed to Baripada and in its place an image of Nṛsiṁhī was installed. Now, the image of Pasachaṇḍī is in active worship in a small shrine next to the Kichakeśvarī temple in the palace compound and is exceptionally well preserved and beautiful. It is not allowed for photography. Stylistically, the image of Nṛsiṁhī of Badasahi and Pedagadi are similar. She is eight-armed and she stands in a slightly flexed pose holding a sword in her major right hand. She is also eating from a *kapāla* held in her left hand. Her lower right hand is in *abhaya-mudrā* while the remaining hands hold a bell and two arrows. In one of her left hands she holds a shield and probably a bow and other one is in *varada-mudrā*. Also an image of Nṛsiṁha is found from the site which is smaller in size and is kept in the Baripada Museum.

N.N. Vasu[36] during his archaeological exploration in Mayurbhanj district noticed the ruins of a stone temple in the eastern part of this village. His account of the temple is noted below. "The temple, although now in ruins, is an object of much interest. If is commonly called the temple of Pasachaṇḍī, a grim skeleton figure with eight arms. The original temple was 6.53 m high and its base 3.65 m. On the roof and columns of the temple is a *vaṭa* tree, grown about 10 feet thick. A glance at the tree will convince one that the temple must have been left neglected for centuries together and consequently fallen into decay. That its artistic beauty was of a high order is evident from the *āmalaka* on the top of the temple. But the plaster having entirely come away there is now no means of forming an idea of its architectural excellence. This stone temple seems to partially indicate the influence of the Dravidian style of architecture and of *khākharā* order's. The original image of Pasachaṇḍī was brought to Baripada and in its place a figure, 91 cm high of Nṛsiṁhī[37] has been substituted. In front of the temple is a courtyard where heaps of stones are lying scattered about. One is tempted to think that these are the ruins of a *naṭamaṇḍapa*. Human skulls having been found here, there is a popular belief that formerly human sacrifice were offered here in large numbers before the goddess. There are traces of the *kurumbera* (enclosure) which existed in early times round the temple and the tank. This *kurumbera* is about 60.80 m square. Formerly on each side of the *Siṁha-dvāra* (lion-gate) there was the figure of a lion standing on elephant. These two figures have now been removed and placed on the courtyard of the temple. The sculptural beauty of the figure of a lion piercing the head of an elephant is superb and admirable. The figures of the goddess and lion are made of chlorite. Stylistically, the image can be assigned to tenth century CE.

Previously, people used to call the place *naramuṇḍa balī* or *balī naramuṇḍa* as numerous human sacrifices used to offer to this goddess. To this fact probably the village owed its name Naramuṇḍīl the place of human sacrifice.[38]

There is a Maṅgala shrine about 65 m from the place on the bank of the Buddhi Pokhari. Other stone idols of the place are a small Jaina *tīrthaṅkara* image seated in *yogāsana* posture, an image of Ambikā, the Śāsanadevī of Nemināthа and one unidentified sculpture displaying sword in the right hand. Some of the local goddesses of the place are Kanaka Durgā, Kālīmāyī, Kotasani, Maṅgalā, Menduasuni, Siṁhavāhinī, Andharī, Ganhaibudi, etc. A place in the outskirts of Badasahi under the name of Barudi is presented by a village deity Kutasuni Ṭhakurānī. Here general terracotta animal figures, temple fragments, a votive Śiva-*liṅgam* and an image of four-armed Ambikā are noticed.

Nahaka Bāhu Temple at Bhitara Kanika

Within the Wild Life Sanctuary at Bhitara Kanika is the renovated Nahaka Bāhu temple, a badly damaged *khākharā* shrine. The presiding deity within the sanctum is an eight-armed Mahiṣamardinī worshipped as Bana-Durgā. Her upper set of hands and the upper part of the back slab are broken up. The image can be dated to the eleventh century. There is also an image of Umā-Maheśvara *mūrti* within the temple. Pārvatī is seated in *ardhaparyaṅka* on the left thigh of Śiva. Erotic images placed near the entrance are later in date.

Gopālinī Temple in the Liṅgarāja Temple Compound at Bhubaneswar

The temple of Gopālinī otherwise known as Bhubaneśvarī, the consort of Lord Liṅgarāja is situated in the Liṅgarāja temple complex at Bhubaneswar (Plate 27). The temple faces towards the east. The presiding deity of the Gopālinī temple is Bhubaneswar or Gopālinī. The main *deula* is of *khākharā* order. There is a legend on *Ekāmra Kṣetra* in *Ekāmra Purāṇa* which runs as follows.

All the sages of the mythological age assembled together and requested Veda Vyāsa to narrate them the significance of *Ekāmra Kṣetra* on the Himāchala[39], the golden mountain and specify its special features according to which Śiva prefers *Ekāmra Kṣetra.* Veda Vyāsa narrated that a sparkling mango tree had itself formed a forest on the bank of the river Gandhabati in *Utkala Deśa* which could bestow truth, wealth, desire and salvation. Pārvatī knew the significance of *Ekāmra Kṣetra* and with the due permission of the Lord Śiva took penance in the guise of Gopāliṇī at *Ekāmra Kṣetra.*[40]

There was a demon king named Mataṅga who had a son called Drinila. Drinila was father of hundred sons and among his hundred sons, Prithluma was the eldest and Kīrti and Vasa were the strongest. These two strong sons, during their stay at *Ekāmra Kṣetra* saw Pārvatī who was living in the guise of a Gopāliṇī and worshiping the *liṅgam* of Gosaleśvara. They wanted to make her their wife. Gopāliṇī informed the ill intention of the demons, so Lord Śiva told about the boon granted to the demons and instructed her to kill them by a treacherous way. Pārvatī suggested that first of all both the demons would carry her on their shoulders and wander about the forest. The demon accepted the suggestion and carried her on their shoulders and then she invoked her *śakti* that bears the burden of the universe as universal mother creator. As a result of this, the demons were killed being pressed under the feet of Gopāliṇī. The scene of killing of the demons has been depicted on the inter-wall of the raised platform of the Gopāliṇī temple.

Plan

On plan the temple is consisted of a *vimāna* and a *jagamohana.* The *Vimāna* is rectangular and *pañcharatha* on plan. It measures 4.90 m by 6.40 m at the base. But the *jagamohana* is square on plan and measured 4.90 m at the base.

Elevation

The *vimāna* has three divisions from bottom to top, viz. *bāḍa, gaṇḍi* and *mastaka.* But the *jagamohana* has four divisions from bottom to top like *piṣṭa, bāḍa, gaṇḍi* and *mastaka.* The height of the temple is approximately 8 m. The main *deula* is built on the ground level. Since, the *vimāna* is not provided with a *piṣṭa* like the *jagamohana,* it is apparent that the *jagamohana* is a later addition. The *jagamohana* is built on a platform of 52 cm height.

Bāḍa

The *bāḍa* portion of the temple has three fold divisions like *pābhāga, jāṅgha* and *baraṇḍa.* The height of the *bāḍa* is 2.25 m. The *pābhāga* of the temple is consisted of four mouldings such as *khūra, kumbha, paṭṭa* and *kani.* Its height is 83 cm. The *jāṅgha* measuring 1.70 m is without any ornamentation. However, the *rāhā* niche on the three sides, which originally housed *pārśva-devatās* are now empty. The size of the niche is about 1 m by 50 cm. The niches are crowned by eave coping. The *baraṇḍa* of the temple is plain and it is consisted of two mouldings.

Gaṇḍi

The *gaṇḍi* of the *deula* is consisted of two tiers. The dividing line of the tiers looks like *kumbha* design. The *rāhā-paga* of the *deula* is progressively narrower towards the top. The *rāhā-paga* of the lower part of *gaṇḍi* is wider than the other two *pagas,* whereas on the upper portion, the *kaṇikā paga* is wider than the *rāhā* and *anuratha paga.* The *gaṇḍi* is bereft of any kind of decoration.

Mastaka

The *mastaka* is crowned by a *kalaśa* and an *āyudha.*

Sanctum

The sanctum of the *vimāna* is dark inside. It is rectangular on plan and plain. The presiding deity is enshrined inside the sanctum.

Doorjamb

The doorjamb of the *vimāna* is decorated with scrollworks. At the lintel portion of the door the image of Gajalakṣmī is carved. The image of the door guard is placed inside the niche at the base of the doorframe on both sides.

Jagamohana

The *jagamohana* is a pyramidal structure. It is built on a low raised platform approached by two steps to enter into the *jagamohana.* The *jāṅgha* of the *jagamohana* is covered with lime plaster. On the *jāṅgha* portion of the *jagamohana* there are three entrances from three directions. The roof is consisted of five *pīḍhas* has or receding tiers. On the top of the fifth *pīḍha* enclosing to the *beki*, there are four *udyatā* lions and four images of seated *devī* known as *mandira carini* to strengthen the *beki* and *āmalaka* of the *mastaka*. There is a large *āmalaka* stone above the *beki*. The *āmalaka* stone is carved with decorative motifs. Above the *āmalaka* are the *khapūri* and lastly the *kalaśa*. The *āyudha* is presently missing which originally must have been a trident, confirming a Śākta shrine.

The temple of Gopāliṇī is assigned to twelfth century CE like other Śākta temples of the Liṅgarāja compound.

Sāvitrī Temple Inside Liṅgarāja Temple Compound at Bhubaneswar

Another temple in the same Liṅgarāja complex of *khākharā* order is that of Sāvitrī, situated in the southern quarter (Plate 28). The temple faces to the east. The temple is a modest construction, without much of carving and ornamentation. Built on the ground without any platform the monument has a *tri-ratha vimāna* fronted by a small *jagamohana.*

Plan

On plan both *vimāna* and *jagamohana* are rectangular and *tri-ratha* corresponding to the three offset projections at the base. The *vimāna* is measuring 2.90 m by 4.10 m externally and 2.30 m by 1.60 m internally al thc base.

Elevation

On vertical elevation it has three fold divisions like *bāḍa, gaṇḍi* and *mastaka*. Its height is about 7 m.

Bāḍa

This temple has *triaṅga bāḍa* or three fold divisions such as *bāḍa gaṇḍi* and *mastaka*. Tbe *pābhāga* of this temple which comprises of three mouldings which are now clearly visible. The height of the *pābhāga* is 48 cm. The *jāṅgha* portion is plain It measures 82 cm in height. On the *rāhā-paga* of the *jāṅgha* there are three niches in the north, east and west sides. The niches are crowned by eave and coping. The niches are now empty. There is no any image in any of the niches.

Gaṇḍi

The main *deula* is divided into two tires. There is an *aṅga-śikhara* on the *rāhā-paga.* The lower portion of the *rāhā-paga* of the main *deula* has become progressively narrower towards the top. The *kaṇikā pagas* are wider than the *rāhā-pagas.*

Mastaka

The *mastaka* of this temple is very strange in composition compared to other Orissan *khākharā* temples. There is the absence of *beki* of the *mastaka.* There is only a *kalaśa* on the *mastaka* and above the *kalaśa* there is *āyudha* as usual.

Sanctum

The sanctum of Sāvitrī temple is rectangular on plan. There is a flight of steps to approach to the sanctum. The presiding deity is enshrined over an earlier pedestal.

Doorjamb

The doorjamb of the Sāvitrī temple is plain. There are two niches at the base of the doorjamb on both sides which contain images of doorguards.

Jagamohana

The *jagamohana* of the temple is in *khākharā* order. It is rectangular and *tri-ratha* on plan. It is fixed with the *vimāna.* The *pābhāga* of the *jagamohana* is much similar to the *vimāna.* The entrance of the *jagamohana* has a small door. There is an *aṅga-śikhara* on the *jāṅgha* portion of the *bāḍa.* The *jagamohana* is progressively narrower towards the top.

Presiding Deity

The presiding deity of the temple is a two-armed *Devī* Sāvitrī. It is later in date the earlier image was probably a Chāmuṇḍā, because, the lower part of the Chāmuṇḍā is still found on the pedestal. The present image is installed over it.

Vārāhī Temple Inside Liṅgarāja Temple Compound at Bhubaneswar

The temple of Vārāhī is in *khākharā* order and *pañcharatha* on plan. It is to the south of Liṅgarāja temple inside the compound of Liṅgarāja (Plate 29) it is facing towards the west. It stands on the same plinth as compared to Liṅgarāja temple. The temple is built of sand stone. The temple is without having *jagamohana*. The temple is now named as Yama temple and the presiding deity Vārāhī is worshiped as Yama.

Plan

On plan the temple is rectangular and *pañcharatha*. It measures 3.10 m by 2.65 m at the base.

Elevation

On vertical elevation the temple had four fold divisions like *piṣṭa, bāḍa, gaṇḍi* and *mastaka*. The *mastaka* portion is totally collapsed. It stands on a low raised platform of 35 cm high.

Bāḍa

It has a *pañcaṅga bāḍa* or five fold divisions like *pābhāga, tala jāṅgha, bandhana, upara jāṅgha* and *baraṇḍa*. The height of the *bāḍa* is 1.65 m. The *pābhāga* is consisted of five usual mouldings like *khūra, kumbha, paṭṭa, kani* and *vasanta*. It measures 40 cm. The mouldings are joined by a vertical rib on each *ratha* projection. The *jāṅgha* portion is devoid of any decoration and the niches are carved on the *tala jāṅgha* portions of the *rāhā* projections. All these niches are empty. The niches are topped by a *pīḍha-muṇḍī* design. The niches measure 20 cm by 40 cm. The *bandhana* of the *bāḍa* has three simple mouldings. The *baraṇḍa* above the upper *jāṅgha* is consisted of four mouldings.

Gaṇḍi

The *gaṇḍi* of the temple is not in a good condition. Probably, there was *vajra-mastaka* design on the front side of the *gaṇḍi*. Projected lion motifs are depicted on the *rāhā-paga* on all the four sides of the *gaṇḍi*.

Mastaka

The *mastaka* portion of the temple is totally ruined.

Sanctum

The sanctum of the temple is rectangular on plan. The presiding deity Vārāhī is depicted on a throne inside the sanctum. But she is worshipped as *Yama.*

Doorjamb

The entrance of the temple is so small that one has to bend down while entering into the temple. There leads a *nandavarta* pedestal to the entrance of the temple. The doorjambs are plain. No Gajalakṣmī image is depicted on the door lintel.

Presiding Deity

The presiding deity of the temple is a Vārāhī image (Plate 30). She is four-armed. Her front right arm is in *abhaya-mudrā.* Her backside right arm is holding a fish. She is holding a baby by her front left arm. Her backside left arm is broken from the elbow probably it held a bowl as found in the cases of most of the Vārāhī images in Orissa. She is seated in *sukhāsana.* She is decorated with different ornaments and her mount buffalo is depicted on the pedestal.

Stylistically, the temple can be dated back to twelfth century CE. Though the presiding deity is an image of Vārāhī, very interestingly, she is worshipped as Yama, the god of death by priests of the temple of Liṅgarāja. Probably, she is mistaken as Yama because of her buffalo mount. As buffalo is also the mount of Yama.

Dakṣiṇa Chaṇḍī Temple at Hadapada

There is a very small *khākharā* order of temple at Hadapada near the Tapang Railway Station in Balapur Mauja in the district of Khurda (Plate 31). It is situated about 2 km from Tapang Railway Station and 20 km from Khurda town towards the south. The temple is facing towards the east. The presiding deity of this temple is a late image of Mahiṣamardinī. She is worshipped as Dakṣiṇa Chaṇḍī by the local people.

Plan

On plan the temple is rectangular and *pañcharatha.* The temple is consisted of a *vimāna,* a *jagamohana* and a high platform. All are placed on the same axial plane. It seems that the *jagamohana* and platforms are later additions. The base of the *vimāna* measures 2.9 m by 4 m internally and 3.23 m by 2.90 m externally.

Elevation

On vertical elevation the temple has four fold divisions like *piṣṭa, bāḍa,* and *mastaka* like most of the Orissan temples. The height of the *vimāna* is 7.60 m. It stands on a platform of 75 cm high.

Bāḍa

The *vimāna* has a *triaṅga bāḍa* or three fold divisions like *pābhāga, jāṅgha* and *baraṇḍa* and also has five vertical segments or *rathas.* The lowest portion of the *bāḍa* or *pābhāga* has four plain mouldings like *khūra, kumbha, paṭṭa* and *kani.* All these mouldings are joined by a vertical rib on each *ratha* divisions. The height of *pābhāga* is 50 cm. The *jāṅgha* has single storeyed design. The *rāhā-pagas* have niches for the placement of the *pārśva-devatās.* The niches are carved within a *rekhā-muṇḍī* which is extended up to the *gaṇḍi* portion. Except some later images the *jāṅgha* portion of the *bāḍa* are plain. A Chinnamastā image is fixed inside the backside *rāhā* niche. Two other *devī* images are placed inside the north and the south niches of the *jāṅgha* portion. The niches measure 39 cm by 62 cm. The niche is crowned by an eave copying. The eave is decorated with lotus petal design. The *baraṇḍa* of the *bāḍa* portion contains two mouldings.

Gaṇḍi

The *gaṇḍi* of the *vimāna* is plain. The *rekhā-muṇḍī* of the *jāṅgha* is extended up to the *gaṇḍi* which is crowned by a *kalaśa* in the north and the south side. But a lion is placed at the top of the backside *muṇḍī.* The *rekhā-muṇḍīs* are *pañcharatha* in design. The *gaṇḍi* is divided into two sections by a thin horizontal recess. An elephant figure is depicted in the north side of the back wall of the *gaṇḍi.* On the front side of the *gaṇḍi* a porch like projection is seen, which is designed like a *khākharā-muṇḍī.*

This type of design is also seen in the Gopālinī and Sāvitrī temples inside the Liṅgarāja temple compound at Bhubaneswar.

Mastaka

The usual elements of the *mastaka* are a *beki*, a big *khākharā* structure, *āmalaka*, *kalaśa*, *āyudha* and *dhvaja*. The *kalaśa* is flanked by two lion figures at the end of both the sides of the *mastaka*.

Sanctum

The sanctum is oblong and dark inside. The *siṁhāsana* of the *Devī* is found against the backside wall. The pedestal of the *siṁhāsana* measures 80 cm by 25 cm. Now marbal plates are fixed on the walls. *Siṁhāsana* is decorated with a band of scrollworks.

Doorjamb

The doorjamb of the *vimāna* is plain. Now iron gates are fixed on both sides. Two door guards are found at the base of the doorjamb on both sides. At the lintel of the doorways the *navagraha* panel is depicted. But interestingly two other images arc found along with *navagraha* images. The image of goddess Lakṣmī is depicted at the centre of lintel just above the doorjamb. The doorway measures 1.40 m by 57 cm. There is a *antarāla* of 58 cm between *vimāna* and *jagamohana*.

Jagamohana

The *jagamohana* of the Dakṣiṇa Chaṇḍī temple is a rectangular structure. It measures 5.30 m by 4.62 m externally and 2.38 m by 1.72 cm internally. The roof of the *jagamohana* is consisted of two tiers and an additional copying is found at the top of the second tier. The eave portion of the *pīḍhas* is decorated with lotus petal motifs. The *bāḍa* portion of the *jagamohana* is plain. It stands on a platform of 70 cm high.

Presiding Deity

The presiding deity under the name Dakṣiṇa Chaṇḍī has been enshrined in a *khākharā* temple at Hadapada in the district of Khurda. The image is a ten-armed

Mahiṣāsuramardinī (Plate 32) carved on the black chlorite stone. The deity in the *pratyālīḍha* state plants her raised left foot on the hind part of the buffalo-carcass and the right foot on the back of the lion-mount.[41] The major right hand of the ferocious goddess plunges a trident held vertically in her front into the chest of the demon who is emerging out of the decapitated body of the buffalo. The uplifted right hand holds a sword while the corresponding left hand holds a shield. The other right hands are represented with a *vajra,* arrow and *chakra.* The remaining left hands are displayed with a *dhanu, nāga* snapping at the head of the demon by enwrapping his neck, axe and a *ghaṇṭā* (bell). A quiver filled with arrows is affixed to the each shoulder of the goddess. The deity wears a girdle and a designed short drapery along with a *vanamālā.* She also wears a beaded necklace, earrings, armlets, wrist-bands and anklets, etc. The goddess is adorned with a *kiriṭamukuṭa.* The hairstyle is beyond description as the head is always besmeared with the vermillion paste. The demon who is well-dressed and bedecked with ornaments holds a long sword in his right hand. The lion appearing from the lower right corner gnaws on the right arm of the demon who is emerging out of the decapitated neck of the buffalo. Here the buffalo with upturned tail is noticed at the lower left corner. This image measures 36 by 20 inches. An inscription which reads as *Narasiṁhadevāṅka navasa aṅka* (Narasiṁhadeva's ninth regnal year) is engraved on the pedestal. On the basis of the epigraphic source the image is assigned to the thirteenth century CE. However, Jayanti Dora in her Ph.D. dissertation (*Sakta Monuments of Orissa,* Utkal University, 2006: 114) has wrongly observed the attributes and mentioned that the image is shown with a mace, lotus, conch and a *kartri* as *āyudhas* on her hands. In the temple complex there are Daśamahāvidyā images enshrined in the small sheds. Goddesss Kālī (Plate 33) is displayed with the sword, severed head and *varada-mudrā* in her hands. Besides a terrific image of the deity Chinnamastā (Plate 34) is found in a small shrine. Her uplifted right hand is shown with a sword and she is decorated with a necklace of human skulls.

Gaṅgeśvarī Temple at Bayalishbati

Gaṅgeśvarī temple is situated in the village of Bayalisbati about two kilometer southeast of Gop in the valley of the Kusabhadra and 16 km from Konark in the district of Puri (Plate 35). It is regarded as the last surviving specimen of *khākharā* order belonging to thirteenth century CE. So, stylistically, it can be related to the Sūrya *deula* of Konark. There is close similarity between the images, particularly erotic motifs of Konark temple and Gaṅgeśvarī temple. According to some local traditions this temple is built by Narasiṁha I. The temple faces towards the south, only few Orissan temples face this direction. This is a major temple of *khākharā* order that exhibits an elaborate scheme of architecture along with extensive carvings in minute details like any other evolved temple of Orissa. The constructional innovations carried for more than five hundred years from eighth century CE bloomed in this temple in all its exuberance.

Plan

The temple consists of a *vimāna* and a *jagamohana.* On plan the *vimāna* of the temple is rectangular and *saptaratha*[42] corresponding to the seven offset projections on each side at the base. The base of the *vimāna* measures approximately 5.72 m by 4.66 m externally and 3.42 m by 2.81 m internally at the bases.[43] The *jagamohana* is *pañcharatha* and square on plan. It measures 6.69 m square at the base.

Elevation

The *vimāna* is of *khākharā* order while the *jagamohana* is a full-fledged *pīḍha* temple. The temple measures 9.42 m in height. On vertical elevation both *vimāna* and *jagamohana* has four divisions like *piṣṭa, bāḍa, gaṇḍi,* and *mastaka.* The temple is erected on a low *piṣṭa* is 25 cm high, partially buried, with a crowning berm and it adheres closely to the outline of the multifaceted plan of the *bāḍa* for both the *deula* and *jagamohana.* The *muhanti* of the berm is relieved with creepers and the centre of each *paga* has a projecting panel decorated with *kiriṭa* designs or with erotic motifs. It is *pañcharatha* on plan and with an additional offset pilaster; it is attached on each side of the *rāhā* as in the Pārvatī temple.

Bāḍa

The vertical *bāḍa* has sub-divisions of *pābhāga, jāṅgha* and *baraṇḍa.* The *pābhāga* is measuring 1.2 m in height consists of five moulding of conventional design like *khūra, kumbha, paṭṭa, kani* and *vasanta.* Here the *vasanta* moulding is relieved with animal procession motif. The *jāṅgha* measures 2.5 m in height. In this portion, the standard *bandhana* has been replaced with panels decorated with *kīrttimukha* masks on the centre facets of the *pagas* and erotic motifs in the *anuratha* recesses. The central projections above the *pābhāga* have each a niche for accommodating *pārśva-devatā.* Each storey is 86 cm in height. The *paga* offsets being relieved with scrollwork runs up to the height of the *jāṅgha* and interrupts the continuity of these two-storey divisions. The major facet of each *paga* is decorated with a *khākharā-muṇḍī* on the lower storey and *pīḍha-muṇḍī* on the upper storey. The *muṇḍī* are *tri-ratha* in style. The *kaṇikā* and *anuratha* of the *jāṅgha* are decorated with creepers and scrollwork having *khākharā-muṇḍī* is at the bottom and *pīḍha-muṇḍīs* of the top relieved with *kīrttimukha* in the middle. The *khākharā-muṇḍī* and *pīḍha-muṇḍīs* of the *kaṇikā* have respectively the figures of *dikpālas* and their *śaktis,* all seated in *lalitāsana* while the *pīḍha-muṇḍī* of *anuratha pagas* enshrine images like Aja-Ekapāda, eight-armed Chāmuṇḍā and four-armed Mahiṣamardinī (Plate 36). The recesses between the projections are carved with the figures of *gajavidala* at the bottom and *mithuna/ maithuna* (erotic) or *alasa-kanyā* motifs at the top.

The *rāhā* is flanked on both sides by a thin pilaster with multiple offsets carved with scrollwork. The pilasters are separated from the major projection by a recess filled with a *vidala* and an *alasa-kanyā.* The frames of the *rāhā* (niche are relieved with scrollwork. The *talagarbhikā* design beneath the niche consists of an elongated *khākharā-muṇḍī.* The *rāhā* design above the niches is missing on all three sides. On the west side there are ruminants of projecting eave mouldings, which probably crowned a larger *pīḍha.* On the top of the *rāhā* the *baraṇḍa* design is replaced by a triple niche which serves as the base for the *vajra-mastaka* of the *gaṇḍi.* The outside niches are filled in with an elephant. All that remains of the *nisa*-shrines are the platform and two large pillars on the west side. These *nisa*-shrines are not the part of the original shrine as evident from the design that the platform is higher than the *piṣṭa* and crowning berm.

The *baraṇḍa* consists of five horizontal mouldings which partake of the *paga* divisions. The *baraṇḍa,* at the top of the *bāḍa* consists of a single moulding, relieved with hanging festoons and a creeper design on its projecting top. However, on the west side near the top of the *rāhā*, the *baraṇḍa* is replaced by a triple niche which is tile base for *viara-mastaka* of the *gaṇḍī*.

Gaṇḍī

The *gaṇḍī* rises to a height of about 10. 33 m. It is arranged in three tiers of four, five and four mouldings respectively. The *gaṇḍī* is designed as *saptaratha* at the base and as *pañcharatha* above. The tires are separated from one another by a recess decorated with plain facets and each tier of the *kaṇikā* and *anuratha* is designed as a *khākharā-muṇḍī* crowned by a *kalaśa*. The tier of the *rāhā* is decorated with a large rectangular panel and flanked by thin multi-faceted pilasters. The panels are decorated with a *vajra-mastaka* consisting of a large double beaded *chaitya* tilled with an elongated *khākharā-muṇḍī* which extends through the recess. The lower tier is decorated with a triple niche while the second tier is designed with scrollwork and is *pañcharatha* in design. It is flanked on each side by a *jāgrata*. The pilasters which flank the *rāhā* terminate at the top of the first *bhūmi* where they are crowned by a *pheṇi* relieved with *padma-prastha*. The *rāhā* on the south or front facade, forming the roof of the *sandhi-sthala*, is more projected and decorated with two *vajra-mastaka* designs. The lower motif is crowned by an *udyatā* lion. The *srahi* is a large spalyed *pheṇi* moulding and it has *paga* divisions of the *gaṇḍī*.

Mastaka

The *beki* portion is plain and the *mastaka* is consisted of a large *khūra*-shaped moulding and is *tri-ratha* in design. The crowning elements are not existed (Plate 37).

Sanctum

The sanctum of the *vimāna* is rectangular on plan and measures 3.42 m by 2.81 m at the base. The *garbhamuda* is resting on eight corbels fastened from four sides. It is further supported by iron beams. A bronze image of Mahiṣamardinī is enshrined on a *siṁhāsana*. There are also free standing pillars at the middle portion to support the ceiling.

Doorjamb

The doorframe of the sanctum is similar in design with the entrance portal of the temple. Here the *dvārapālas* have one leg uplifted and they hold a mace in front of their body, they bow their heads down ward resting on the lotus cushion, with one arm crossed in front of the body resting on the weapon while the other hand rose in *abhaya-mudrā*. The hair of both *dvārapālas* is arranged in serpent like coils. Beneath the *dvārapāla*, flanking the *nandavarta* step are seated figures. The lintel is designed as *pīḍha-muṇḍī* and is carved with Gajalakṣmī in geese and resting on a pedestal. As mentioned in the work of Devala Mitra this is an image of Gaṅgeśvarī.

The *sandhi-sthala* is decorated with a *paga* and a pilaster which has a single storey plan and connected the sanctum with *jagamohana*. The *paga* is designed as an elongated *khākharā-muṇḍī*. The niche of the *khākharā-muṇḍī* contains two superimposed panels of figure motifs carved in low-relief. The recess separating the *paga* from the *deula* contains a *vidala* and a *maithuna* in a two storeyed design.

Jagamohana

The *jagamohana, pañcharatha* on plan is a *pīḍha deula*. It is standing on a platform. The *pābhāga* is 84 cm in height. It consists of five mouldings such as *khūra, kumbha. paṭṭa, kani* and *vasanta*. But it is clearly visible only on *paga* offsets and on the pilasters forming the base of the *toraṇas* decorating the entrance portal and window projection. It consists a multifaceted, *khākharā-muṇḍī* flanked by a *nāga-nāgī stambha* on each side with a double *gajakrānta* at the base of each *stambha*.

The *tri-ratha* division of the *pābhāga* continues on the *jāṅgha* where the *muṇḍīs* are flanked by thin *vajra-stambhas* and the *kīrttimukha* panel by a flat *stambha*. The *vajra-stambhas* are decorated with a standing female figure in a niche crowned by a *vajra-mastaka*. Here the *jāṅgha* has two storey designs, of which the lower storey has *khākharā-muṇḍī* of 66 cm high and upper storey is designed as truncated *pīḍha-muṇḍī* 59 cm in height. The *pīḍha-muṇḍī* is crowned by a sculptured panel flanked by, an ntid figure carved on the *stambhas*. The *muṇḍī* niches are flanked by a thin pillar each side. The niches of the *kaṇikā* are housing the *dikpālas* and their *śaktis* while niches of the *anuratha* are housing the images of *Śaiva* and *Śākta* pantheons. The ses of *anuratha* are filled with *vidala* motifs on the lower storey and *alasa-kanyā* or *maithuna* motifs on the upper storey. The *jāṅgha* portion of the *jagamohana* consists of super imposed rows of sculptured panels where as the *pābhāga* and *baraṇḍa* are designed as multi-faceted structures.

The *gaṇḍi* is *pañcharatha* and pyramidal in style. It is so arranged that each tier is separated by a recess. The lower tier is having four *pīḍha*-mouldings, while the damaged upper tier has a brick core. The projecting lower tier over the *gavākṣa* is crowned by an *āmalaka* with surmounting *udyatā* lion.

The ceiling inside the *jagamohana* is a dome with ten circular corbels capped by a small disc simulating a lotus medallion though lacking detailed ornamentation. The lowest corbel rests on an octagon formed by the middle portions of the walls and four beams spanning the corners of the *jagamohana*.

The entrance portal on the south projects about 1.52 m, including the *toraṇa*, with the lateral flanks decorated with a *paga* division and a thin pilaster, both having a *pābhāga* of five mouldings rather than a *talagarbhikā* design. The pilaster is decorated with scrollwork and the *paga* has two *muṇḍīs* divided by a *kīrttimukha*. Above it, the *baraṇḍa* is eliminated and replaced by a large framed niche decorated with a *śikṣādāna* motif on both the east and west sides. The base of the pillars supporting the arch of the *toraṇa* is carved as a *pābhāga* with five mouldings and the shaft is 16 sided and decorated with scrollwork. It is separated into two storeyes by raised horizontal ridges, along with an *alamba* motif of *kīrttimukha* mask with dripping festoons at the top. The capital consists of a *khūra* surmounted by a *pheṇi* at the top. The arch is ornately decorated with scrollwork and has recessed facets inside wall. At the base of the major facet there is a guardian figure on each side while on the outside there is *makara* figure. The arch frames an image of Aja-Ekapāda carved above the architrave and extends up the height of the first *bhūmi* of the *pīḍha*-roof it is surmounted by a projecting lion figure.

The doorframe of the *jagamohana* is decorated with three bands of scrollwork like *kuṭilā*, *gelaba* and intertwining *nāga*. The base of the jambs has *pīḍha-muṇḍī* which houses the *dvārapālas*. The *dvārapālas* stand in a *samabhaṅga* pose holding the trident in their left hand. The benign *dvārapāla* on the proper right wears a high *tiara*. But terrifying companion on the left, stout in body proportions has his hair arranged in three pointed braids surrounded by a serpent-hooded halo. Beneath the *dvārapālas*, flanking the plain *nandavarta* step there is a panel of scrollwork. An image of Gajalakṣmī is carved on the lintel while the *navagrahas* are on a projecting slab. At the apex of the *toraṇa* design there is an Aja-Ekapāda image.

On the *gavākṣa* projections the shaft of the pillars is round but plain, but an *alamba* her motif appears at the top. The arch is trefoil and without capital. All of its facets are decorated with scrollwork and a small guardian figure is found at the base along with projecting *makaras*. Within the niche frame by the arch there is a standing Kārttikeya in the east and a seated four-armed goddess in the west. At the top of the arch, there is a *kīrttimukha* mask. The arch is ended beneath the projecting *pīḍha* roof.

The *gavākṣa* window is framed by bands of scrollwork and filed with three balusters, each baluster containing an *alasa-kanyā* carved in high relief. Below the window there is a *talagarbhikā* consisting of a multi-faceted *khākharā-muṇḍī* flanked on each side by a *nāga-nāgī stambha* with double *gajakrānta* at its base. The lintel is decorated with elephant frieze. The *gavākṣa* projections and entrance portal are each framed by a large *makara-toraṇa* with more ornate design. The arch of the entrance is pentafoil in shape.

Cult Images

Among the major cult images, Gaṇeśa in the west and Vārāhī in the east are still in *situ*. The image of four-armed Gaṇeśa carved of khondalite stone sits on a lotus and holds the *kuthara, modaka pātra*, broken-tusk and rosary. A trefoil-shaped *toraṇa* frames the head of Gaṇeśa with a *kīrttimukha* at the apex and garland-bearing females in the upper corners. His mount mouse looks up at him from the pedestal on the right. There is an attendant appearing in each lower corner.

The image of Vārāhī, made out of chlorite is really impressive although her snout is almost missing. She is standing in a slightly flexed pose licking blood from a cup held in her major left hand. In her other hands she holds a *karti*, a shield and a club. Her body ornamentation, particularly the girdle or *mekhala* is exquisitely carved. Her coiffure consists of rows of serpent-coils rising like flames. She is flanked on either side by a small duplicate image of herself. The upper corners of the back-slab are decorated with flying *vidyādhara* on each side and beneath each one there is a pair of *haṁsa*, with garlands dripping from their beaks.

The empty niche in the north side is filled in with a warrior riding on a pouncing horse. His hair is arranged in serpentine coils and he lifts a sword in his right hand. Probably the original image for the niche is Pārvatī. That may be the one headless figure of Pārvatī which is lying inside the *jagamohana*. Stylistically, she is similar to Vārāhī image. In her lower hands she holds a rosary and a lotus stalk and in her uplifted hands, holds an *aṅkuśa* and a *nāga-pāśa*. She is flanked on both sides by an attendant holding an *aṅkuśa* and a *nāga-pāśa* and a lion-mount is there on the right side of the pedestal.

The *dikpālas* and *dikpālikās*, on both the *deula* and the *jagamohana*, are all seated in *lalitāsana* on their respective mounts in the traditional manner.

The *anuratha* niches of the *deula* house images of *Mahāvidyās* along with an image of Ekapāda Śiva, the later appearing on the upper north *anuratha* in the east side. As the stone are of bad quality most of the images are damaged. One of the important cult images is Mahiṣamardinī depicted on the lower south *anuratha paga* of the east side. She is four-armed and she plunges the trident held in her major two hands into the neck of the demon attempting to escape from the buffalo-carcass and her upper right and left hands hold a sword and a club respectively. There is also an image of emaciated Chāmuṇḍā in the east lower *anuratha* on the north side and possibly another Mahiṣamardinī image is there in the upper niche of the same *paga* an eight-armed Chāmuṇḍā is depicted as dancing on a corpse. She holds a sword over her head with her major right hand while the major left hand holds a *kapāla* in front of her chest. One of her hands holds a shield and another hand holds severed head appears in the upper left corner of the niche.

There is another six-armed figure of the same type, though not emaciated which is represented in *pratyālīḍha* with the right leg forward and slightly bent, placed on a corpse on the pedestal in the lower north *anuratha paga* of the west side. The major right hand lifts a sword above the head and the major left hand holds a *kapāla* in front of the chest. The objects held in the lower hands do not exist and the upper hands hold a trident and a *ḍamaru* to suggest her link with Śaivism. Other figures have four or six arms while one of them has three heads.

The cult images of the *anuratha* niches on the *jagamohana* are various male and female deities of the Śaiva and Śākta pantheons and are depicted as seated on lotus cushion. There is only one standing image of the six-armed Gaṇeśa in the lower east *anuratha* niche on the south side. He holds a serpent above his head with his upper two hands. His major two hands hold a broken tusk and a *modaka pātra* while his lower hands hold a rosary and probably a *kuthara.* He stands in a slightly flexed pose and his mount mouse looks up at him from the lower right corner. Most of the male and female figures and deities are seated in *lalitāsana,* holding a *vīṇā,* with their major two hands. Probably, they are the images of Vīrabhadra or Vīṇādhara Śiva and Sarasvatī. There are also Durgā and Hara-Pārvatī images. There is also an image, in the upper niche on the east flank of the entrance portal, of *liṅgam-pūjā* with two emaciated ascetics pouring libations over a *mukhaliṅgam* placed on the back of the bull Nandī. In the lower south *anuratha* in the west side there is an unusual image in meditative pose with folding hands. Five serpent heads form a canopy is there over his head and seven jars are also there on his pedestal.

Within a small hut at a short distance towards the east of the temple there is a four-armed image of Mahiṣamardinī, killing the buffalo-demon. The goddess stands with one foot on the back of her lion-mount and the other on the back of the buffalo-carcass, while plunging the trident into the demon. She holds the trident in her two major hands. Her upper right hand holds a sword and the back left hand holds a bell. The image is slightly smaller than the *pārśva-devatās,* may be of later date and not ornately carved. The pedestal is also plain. There are other two small bronze images, one is in the hut and the other is on the *vedi* inside the same temple and with similar iconography features.[44]

Decorative Motifs

All the *muṇḍī* niches are being occupied by *dikpālas* and their, *śaktis* or by various deities of the Śaiva and Śākta pantheon. But the decorative figure motifs of the upper storey recesses are the *alasa-kanyās* and *mithuna* or *maithuna* motifs, most of which are now missing. In the *sandhi-sthala* there is an image, where in, the female is represented as mounting or climbing on the male who is standing against the wall similar to examples of Konark and on other early thirteenth century temples. The most noticeable of the erotic motifs remaining are those carved on the panels placed in the recesses forming a *bandhana* with the *kīrttimukha* masks of the *pagas,* the band contains erotic motifs of which run continuously around the temple. There is also a scene of hair cutting and on the face of the berm crowning the *piṣṭa,* there is the popular motif of a male figure embracing a female. There are also some surviving *alasa-kanyā* images, the best-preserved being those on the balusters of the *gavākṣa* windows. Female figures like *cauri*-bearers are carved on the *stambhas* flanking the *muṇḍīs.* There are also many small images of female figures housed in the niches of the *talagarbhikā* designs of the *pābhāga.*

Apart from erotic imagery, the most popular motifs include the *śikṣādāna,* with a *guru* and royal figure among disciples or followers, and military or hunting scenes. The largest of the *śikṣādāna* motifs is that replacing the *baraṇḍa* on the east and west lateral flanks of the entrance portal on the south side of the *jagamohana.* As the best-preserved example, on the west, there is a scene which represents a royal personage seated on a low couch, supported by jars, with one leg crossed and a pillow placed behind his back. He faces towards three rows of figures much smaller in size, which stand with hands folded in *añjalī* in the lower two rows and hold a *chauri* over the shoulder in the top row. Aligned with these figures of the top row, there is a female figure that probably represents his wife. In the upper left corner, behind the king, a figure of an attendant is there. The scene on the east side is similar though these figures are bringing gifts and the seated figure may be of a female. The figure closest to the queen is seated on the floor with hands folded in *añjalī* and an object held against the body with one arm. Both scenes are framed by a band of *vartula* scrollwork. There are also numerous smaller *sikhadana* scenes appearing on the panel crowning the upper storey *muṇḍī* on the *pagas* of the *jagamohana.* Generally, these panels are decorated with military or hunting scenes with figures on horseback or as walking. In one scene, the hunter has held a lion by its throat; the lion is standing on its hind legs, while the hunter is holding a knife above his head with his uplifted right hand. These panels are flanked by atlíntid figures who generally assume the same bent-knee posture suggestive of running or flying.

The *vidala* motifs filling the lower recesses are not varied in treatment as at Konark, being confined in narrow quarters, and are rendered riderless. The striking or unique decorative motif is the *kīrttimukha* masks serving as a *bandhana* element to divide the *pagas* into two storeys. Each mask is vigorously carved on a panel with beaded borders as independent motifs, laying with the images enshrined within the *muṇḍī* niches for importance, rather than forming part of a minor decorative frieze (*alamba*) in the traditional manner. The mask represents a close-up flattened view dominated by long horns, bulging eyes and grinning mouth with mustache and the face cut off at the lower lip. The *nāga-stambhas* have only one serpent each in the conventional manner though the *gajakrānta* motifs at the base are more varied in treatment than in earlier temples. The most popular scroll motifs are the *vanalatā*, *vartula* with the *padma-pṛstha* and the *nāga-bandha* with intertwining serpent which appears on the door frame. But the perforated *jālī* pattern so popular at Konark are not used as decorative motif in this temple.

Presiding Deity

The presiding deity of the temple is a four-armed Mahiṣamardinī (Plate 38). The goddess is carved on a very beautiful masonry pedestal with a decorative toraṇa as the jambs framing the niche. The deity is standing in a *saumya* posture. Her major right hand plunges a trident into the chest of the demon in human form while the major left hand holds an object (probably the hair of the demon) which is indistinct. The uplifted right hand is represented with a sword and the corresponding left hand holds a bell. The Devī wears the standard body ornamentation such as *patra- kuṇḍala*, necklace, armlets and a designed girdle along with a short drapery. She is also crowned with a *kiriṭamukuṭa* head-gear. The mount lion appearing from the right corner attacks the demon. The female attendant equipped with weapons is found on the either side of the goddess. This image is assigned to the thirteenth century CE on the basis of the temple architecture. Moreover, on the eastern side of the Gaṅgeśvarī temple, a deity with four arms has been housed in a thatched hut. Her uplifted left leg is planted on the back of the buffalo-carcass and right-foot on the mount-lion, contrary to the conventional iconography. Like the image of Motia the trident held vertically in front of her body with major hands plunges into the chest of the demon. The uplifted right hand is shown with a sword while the back left hand with a bell. She has a *patra-kuṇḍala* in each of her ear. She also puts on a conical crown. The attempt of the demon for pulling a sword from a scabbard is prevented by the lion. The image measures 34 by 20 inches. It is assigned to last half of the thirteenth century CE. Two small bronze images of the similar rapture are also housed in the same hut.

It is recorded in the *Baya Chakada* that during the 18th *aṅka* of Nṛsiṁha, at the time of the closing of the *deula* work camp, 12 bullock cartloads of small stones were sent to the Gaṅgeśvarī *devī* of Bayalisbati and that Dharma Mahapatra, the son of the *Sūtradhāra* of the Sūrya *deula*, measured out the temple. This account places the construction of the temple immediately following the completion of the Sun temple in about 1260 CE. Further it is seen that architecturally as well as stylistically, this temple has close similarities with the famous Konark temple, hence it can safely be assigned to thirteenth century CE.

The above discussion shows that in total there are nineteen extant *khākharā* temples in Orissa from eighth century to thirteenth century CE, out of which eleven are in good condition, three are renovated and the rest five are in dilapidated condition. All these temples are spread over the districts like Balasore, Ganjam, Khurda, Kalahandi and Puri. The *khākharā* temples which generally contain the female divinities thus play a vital role in the history of temple building activities of Orissa by glorifying the cultural heritage not only of Orissa but also of our subcontinent in general.

References

1. Priyabala Shah (ed.), *Viṣṇudharamottara Purāṇa*, Baroda, 1953, pp. 231-232.
2. D. Mitra, *JASB*, 11, p. 23.
3. Alice Borner and Sadasiva Ratha Sarma, *Principles of Composition in Hindu Sculptures*, Delhi, 1985, pp. XXXI-XIII.
4. *Ibid.*
5. *Ibid.*
6. N.K. Bose, *Orissan Temple Architecture*, Delhi, 2001, p. XIV.
7. *Ibid.*
8. D. Mitra, *JASB*, 11, pp. 1-3.
9. *Ibid.*, p. 2.
10. N.K. Bose, *op.ct.*, pp. 171-73.
11. K.C. Panigrahi, Bhauma Art and Architecture of Orissa, *A.A.*, vol. I, 1957, pp. 98-99.

12. *Ibid.*
13. T.E. Donaldson, *op. cit.,* vol. I, 1987, pp. 98-99.
14. *Ibid.,* pp. 101-102.
15. D. Mitra, *op. cit.,* p. 33.
16. K.C. Panigrahi, *op. cit.,* pp. 78-80.
17. *Ibid.*
18. J.N. Banerjee, *Development of Hindu Iconography,* Calcutta, 1956, pp. 78-80.
19. John Fleet, Allahabad Pillar Inscription of Samudragupta, *C.I.I,* vol. III, 1970, pp. 72-79.
20. The inscription consists of a single line reads "*oṁ śrī chāmundra udaḥ*", K.C. Panigrahi, *op. cit.,* pp. 32-33.
21. *E.I.,* vol. XVII, p. 253.
22. T.E. Donaldson, *op. cit.,* p. 183.
23. R.P. Mahapatra, *Archaeology in Orissa,* Delhi, 1986, vol. II, p. 103.
24. H.C. Das, *Śākta Pīṭhas: A Study,* Bhubaneswar, 1999, p. 57.
25. K. Acharya, *Ekāmra Kshrtea, Bhubaneswar,* in Utkal Pathak Sansad, Kedar Gouri (ed.), Cuttack, 1993, p. 338.
26. D. Mitra, *op. cit.,* p. 45.
27. The *mastaka* is a recent construction. Efforts were to maintain its original shape at the time of restoration. It looks white because of original shape at the time of restoration. It looks white because of white-washing.
28. O.C. Ganguly and A. Goswami, *Orissan Sculpture and Architecture,* Calcutta, 1956, p. 7.
29. T.E. Donaldson, *op. cit.,* p. 294.
30. K.C. Panigrahi, *op. cit.,* pp. 248-249.
31. D. Mitra, *JAS,* vol. II, p. 3.
32. P.K. Ray, *op. cit.,* 1984-75, Bhubaneswar, 1975.
33. A Boner and S. Ratha Sharma, *op. cit.,* XXI.

34. He is a *Yogin,* a naked ascetic with matted hair, covered with ashes, A. Boner and S.R. Sharma, *op. cit.,* p. XLIII.

35. According to the *Kamakalavilasathe āvaraṇa śaktis* are like the limbs of the supreme *Śakti,* when she changes into the *chakra,*or like her rays, when her effulgence goes into manifestation. "She is then represented as the *Śrīchakra,* the *yantra* of nine triangles". A. Boner and S.R. Sharma, *op. cit.*, p. XLIV.

36. N.N. Vasu, *op. cit.*

37. N. Senapati and N.K. Sahu (eds.), *Mayurbhanj District Gazetteer,* Cuttack, 1967, pp. 458-461.

38. *Ibid.,* pp. 458-461.

39. R.K. Das, *Temple of Tamilnadu,* Bombay, 1964, pp. 49-50.

40. *Ibid.*

41. Sanjaya Kumar Mahapatra, *Mahiṣāsuramardinī in Art, Iconography and Cult Practices,* Agam Kala Prakashan, Delhi, 2014, p. 87.

42. According to H.C. Das it is *Saptaratha,* while T.E. Donaldson states that it is *pañcharatha.* H.C. Das, *op. cit.*, p. 60; T.E. Donaldson, *op. cit.*, vol. II, p. 629. In fact it is *saptaratha* on plan.

43. D. Mitra, *JASB,* vol. II, 1960, p. 8.

44. *Ibid.,* p. 10.

Chapter VI
Conclusion

Situated on the cross-road between north and south, Orissa is characteristically the meeting ground of various waves of religious faiths and believes. It is not only witnessed the migration of Āryan culture from north to south but also harbored great religions and cults like Buddhism, Jainism, Vaiṣṇavism, Śaivism and Śaktism with equal resilience and ease. The religious history of Orissa had close associates with the political development of the land from the earliest times. During the early centuries of the Christian Era it was characterized by small territorial units under various names such as Kaliṅga, Kaṅgoda, Dakṣiṇa Kosala, Tosali (*uttarā* and *dakṣiṇa*) along with their dependencies like the *maṇḍala* states namely *Khiñjalī-maṇḍala, Kodalaka-maṇḍala, Bonai-maṇḍala, Khijiṅga-maṇḍala,* etc. being separated from each other through a network of mountains and river systems and populated mostly by the primitive tribes. Jainism and Buddhism flourished in Orissa along with Brahmanical religious faiths like Śaivism, Vaiṣṇavism and Śaktism under the benign patronage of various royal dynasties like Śailodbhavas, Bhauma-Karas, Pāṇḍuvaṁśīs, Kalachuries, Somavaṁśīs, Imperial Gaṅgas and Sūryavaṁśī Gajapatis who ruled over the land in succession. The eclectic religious temperament of the rulers led to the peaceful co-existence of all major religious faiths like Brahmanism, Buddhism and Jainism as attested to by the religious vestiges and archaeological remains found throughout the state.

Temple is the most significant and characteristic product of Indian architecture and is reckoned among the oldest institutions of India. Since Gupta period a large number of temples were constructed all over India to enshrine the deities of Hindu pantheon. To serve the ritualistic requirements, the early Indian temples comprised of a sanctum for housing the presiding deity and a small pillared porch for sheltering the worshippers which subsequently became a complex structure in conformity with the elaborate Hindu practices.

The temples constructed in Orissa to enshrine the deities in the post-Gupta period are pronounced with individualistic and variegated characteristics at the hands of Kaliṅgan craftsmen. Developed as a distinct class of architecture known as Kaliṅgan style as mentioned in the *Śilpa* text like *Bhubana pradīpa, Śilpa Prakāśa* and *Śilparanakośa* and epigraphic records (Amṛteśvara temple inscription). The *Śilpa* texts of Orissa prescribe three types of temples, *rekhā, pīḍha* and *khākharā.* These three categories are also clearly discernible among the extant temples of Orissa. The temple building activities pursued for more than seven hundred years from 5th-6th to the thirteenth centuries CE, led to the proliferation of hundreds of temples throughout the length and breadth of the state.

The temples of Orissa were built mostly of sandstone or khandolite. But some temples are also built of laterite stone like the Mahiṣamardinī temple at Sergarh, Chaṇḍī temple at Kishorepur, etc. Huge blocks of stones were transported by land and river form the quarry sites to the places of construction. These stones were laid dry, evenly and horizontally one upon the other and kept in position largely by their own solid weight and by their even balance. In crucial points iron dowels were used. It was an all together dry machinery that was in practice for building temples of stone.

On plan, the Śākta temples, particularly the *khākharā* order consisted an oblong (rectangular) sanctum and a *jagamohana* (frontal hall of *pīḍha* order being connected by a *antarāla* (vestible). However, departures are noticed in the temples like the unique Chausathi Yoginī temple at Ranipur-Jharial and Hirapur, whose ground plan are circular. On elevation in some cases the temples are created on a *piṣṭa* or a platform upon which the temple proper is constructed, which has three fold divisions vertically from the base to the finial such as *bāḍa*, *gaṇḍi* and *mastaka*. The survey reveals that up to the *bāḍa* or the wall portions architectural designs are almost the same with that of *rekhā* and *pīḍha* temples, while they are characterized otherwise by their respective *gaṇḍi*. According to Percy Brown *khākharā* temples are probably influenced by the *gopuram* style of south Indian temples art traditions which may not be accepted on account of its chronological preference. In Orissa there is a local experimentation on the *nāgara* style of north Indian temple art tradition in the hand of Orissan artist. Such an order was very likely devised and evolved due to the practical need of the ritual of this cult.

Taking into account the architectural features of the *mastaka* the *khākharā* temples of Orissa can be sub-divided into three categories. The survey bring out that nowhere in India temples of *khākharā* order are exclusively dedicated to Śākta deities as Orissa. This indicate that though the Orissan artists were influenced by the Gupta art traditions of north and central India and the Dravidian style of the south, they maintained their individuality and produced an unique variety of temple style. It is also important to note the style that was conceived and evolved here came to us in its complete and finest form without any trace of its rudimentary beginning or experimentations. One of the beautiful and earliest among the extant *khākharā* temples is the Vaitāl *deula* at Bhubaneswar that belonged to eighth century CE and enshrined goddess Chāmuṇḍā. Subsequently, we come across a numbers of *khākharā* temples dedicated to the Śākta goddess. The smallest temple of this variety is the smaller *khākharā* shrine at Ranipur-Jharial, while the biggest one is the Gaṅgeśvarī temple at Bayalisbati. The last construction of the classical idiom was also the Gaṅgeśvarī temple at Bayalisbati erected in thirteenth century CE that enshrined the deity Gaṅgeśvarī, in the form of Mahiṣamardinī, which is one of the finest products of the Gaṅga period at the last phase of canonical temple building in Orissa. Due to its artistic excellence it has earned the reputation as "Mini Konark". Between these two milestones of *khākharā* order several *khākharā* temples have been built for Śākta deities during the period from the eighth century to the thirteenth century CE.

It is a common feature that *khākharā* types of temples are rectangular on plan. But, there is the exception of this rule in case of Nārāyaṇī temple at Chilika. The temple is square on plan. Another interesting feature of this temple is that it is built of monolith like the *rathas* of Mahabalipuram. Even the *pārśva-devatā* images and the presiding deities are carved out of the same stone along with the temple. Usually at the top of the *mastaka* two lion figures flanked the *kalaśa,* but in case of Nārāyaṇī two elephant figures are represented at the top of the *mastaka* on both sides of the *kalaśa.*

Another interesting feature of the *khākharā* shrine is its wide usage as a decorative motif in the *jāṅgha* portion of the *rekhā, pīḍha* and *khākharā deula.* Designed as a miniature shrine in relief on the *bāḍa* portion, it not only adds to the beauty of the temple proper but also serves as a frame to accommodate the cult images carved on the wall of the temple. Canonically, it was termed as *khākharā-muṇḍī.* A close scrutiny of Vaitāl *deula* reveals that the *khākharā* motif crowned by a *vajra-muṇḍī* on the sidewalls that characterized the *gaṇḍi* portion of the temple is an imitation of the temple proper. It is difficult to say whether the temple inspired the motif or the *vice-versa* since both the examples are noticed in the earliest known Vaitāl temple of *khākharā* order. With the development of a two-storeyed elevation for the *jāṅgha* the *khākharā-muṇḍī* becomes the standard motif/design for the lower storey of the subsidiary *pagas.*

Orissa unlike many other parts of India has the prized distinction of possessing an uninterrupted series of temples illustrating the inception to decline. To add more, temples constitute the most dominant form of architecture in Orissa. Above all the *khākharā* temples occupy a very significant place in the sphere of art and architecture of Orissa right from the beginning of the temples building activities in the state. These temples form one of the most compact and homogenous architectural groups in India.

Glossary

Āgama	Relating to Tantricism, scroll motif with circular vartula vines alternating with foliage of freshly sprouted mustard.
Agni	Fire.
Ākāśaliṅgam	*liṅgam* (phallic) shaped finial surmounting the *mastaka* of early Śaiva temples.
Alasa-kanyā	Indolent or playful damsel; female figures in various poses decorating the walls of temples.
Āliṅgana	An embrace.
āmalaka, āmalā	Fluted disc resembling an *āmalaka* fruit (emblic myrobalan), which resting on the beki forms an important component of the *mastaka* of a *rekhā* or a *pīḍhā* temple; *bhūmi-āmalā* similar member demarcating one *bhūmi* from another in the *kaṇikā paga* of the *rekhā* temple.
Aṅga	Part of body.
Aṅga-śikhara	Miniature representation of the *rekhā* shrine on the spire of a temple.
Anuraha	Narrow vertical recess separating *pagas*.

Aṣṭadikpāla	Guardians of eight (four cardinal and four intermediate) quarters.
Āvaraṇa-devatā	Secondary deities surrounding the main presiding deity of the temple, forming a protective ring; they usually occupy the *anuratha* niches.
Avatāra	Incarnations of gods and goddess.
Bāḍa	Wall or vertical portion of the temple above *piṣṭa* (platform) and below the curvilinear, pyramidal spire or barrel vaulted super structure.
Bahana/Vāhana	Mount of gods and goddesses.
Bandhana	Stringcourse: series of horizontal mouldings along a wall.
Baṅka-jālī	Lattice.
Baraṇḍa	Horizontal platforms forming top element divisions on the *bāḍa*.
Baraṇḍi	Horizontal platforms forming *bhūmi* divisions on the *gaṇḍi*.
Basanta	Top most moulding of human being.
Beki	Neck of the temple between the spire and the *āmalaka* or *mastaka*.
Bhadra	Auspicious, *pīḍhā* deula, *mukhaśālā* in front of the temple.
Bhōgamaṇḍapa	Hall of offering or refectory or refectory hall of a temple.
Bhūmi	Storey plane, storeyed division of the *kaṇikā paga* of the *gaṇḍi* of a *rekhā deula*; *bhūmi-āmalā* see *āmalā*.
Bisama/viṣama	Topmost course of the *gaṇḍi*, just below the *beki*.
Chaitya	Ornamental motif in the shape of a stylized horse shoe.
Dakṣiṇa	South.
Deula	Sanctuary, general name for a temple.
Deula chāriṇī	Female figures find at the *beki* portion of the temple.
Devas	Gods.

Devī	Goddess.
Dhama	Religious centre.
Dhvaja	Flag, banner, final.
Dikpālas	Guardians of the eight quarters, *Lokapālas.*
Dopichihha siṁha	A lion with two hind parts at right angles to each other.
Dvārapāla	Door-keeper.
Dvārapālikā	Female door-keeper.
Gaja	Elephant.
Gajakrānta	Motif of a lion springing on the back of an elephant; *gaja-siṁha.*
Gaṇḍi	"Trunk"; curvilinear spire or pyramidal roof above the *bāḍa śikhara.*
Garbhagṛha	Sanctum, womb of a temple or inter most chamber.
Garbhamuṇḍa	Lowest ceiling of the sanctum.
Gavākṣa	Window.
Gelaba	Scrollwork of boys climbing a meandering vine.
Ghaṇṭā	Bell, bell-shaped member in the final of *pīḍhā deula.*
Hasta	Hand, arm.
Īśvara	Lord.
Jagamohana	Rectangular or square hall or porch infront of the sanctum, *mukhaśālā.*
Jalapātra	Scroll motif or superimposed water plants.
Jālī	Any perforated or honeycombed pattern.
Jāṅgha	'shin', a vertical portion of the *bāḍa* between the *pābhāga* and the *baraṇḍa.*
Jhapasiṁha	Rampant lion.
Jñāna	Supreme knowledge; spiritual knowledge; transcendental insight.

Kalaśa	Water pot, pitcher-shaped member in the final of a temple.
Kani	Moulding of the shape of 'V' placed sideways.
Kaṇṭhi	Veritical recess between moulding, *pīḍhās* or *potalas.*
Khākharā	Semi-cylindrical member resembling the local vegetable boiti *kākharu* (pumpkin gourd).
Khākharā Deula	Temple having a *khākharā* structure (barrel vaulted roof) as the crowning member. It is always dedicated to some form of *śakti* and oblong on plan.
Khākharā-muṇḍī	Miniature representation of *khākharā* temple carved as decorative motify on the *pagas.*
Khapuri	Skull, flattish bell shaped member above the *āmla.*
Khūra	*Cyma recta;* first basic element of *pābhāga* in the form of a hoof.
Kumbha	Water-pot also moulding having the profile of a water pot.
Liṅgam	The phallic emblem of Śiva, male generative organ.
Mashya bandhana	Stringing course in the middle of the *jāṅgha* portion of the *bāḍa.*
Maithuna	Sexual intercourse.
Makaratoraṇa	*Toraṇa* (arch) with a *makara* on each side at the base of arch while a *kīrttimukha* is generally at the apex.
Maṇḍapa	Hall in front of the main shrine.
Mandira	Temple.
Mandira chāriṇī	Figure squatting on its hunches frequently placed on the pedestal of a deity.
Mastaka	Crowing elements above the spire or *gaṇḍi;* head.
Muhanti	Projecting fillet at the base of a *khūra, pīḍhā, khākharā,* also short vertical portion at the base of a *khūra, pīḍhā* and *khākharā* structure.

Mukhaśālā	Frontal hall, fontal porch.
Muṇḍī	Miniature temple, carved on wall as a decorative motif.
Nadir	Central point inside the plinth of the temple where the great serpent Ananta remains.
Navagraha	Planet slab on the architrave of the portal with nine planetary representation.
Nāyikā	Female figures in various poses and actions on the walls of the temple.
Pābhāga	A set of moulding constituting the lowest part of the *bāḍa*.
Paga	Vertical projections of the *bāḍa* and *gaṇḍi* of the temple *ratha*.
Pañchāyantana	Five shrined complex with small shrines at the four corner of the compound with main temple at the center.
Pārśva-devatā	Accessory deity occupying the niches of the central projection (*rāhā*) of main temple. They very according to the religious association of the temple/presiding deity.
Paṭṭa	Flange, plain broad stone band.
Pīḍhā	Flattish wooden seat, projecting members constituting the pyramidal roof of a *pīḍhā*.
Piṣṭa deula	Temple with a roof made of *pīḍhās* aligned in steps dorming a pyramidal silhouette. This form is generally limited to the *jagamohana, bhōgamaṇḍapa* and *naṭamaṇḍapa*.
Prakṛti	Cosmic substance; the uncaused cause of phenomenal existences; nature.
Pratiratha	The thin *paga* inserted between major *paga* on *saptaratha* and *navaratha* planned temple.
Rāhā	Central vertical projection on the *deula*.
Rathas	Vertical projection of the temple, *paga*, temple car; chariot.
Rekhā	Curvilinear spire.

Rekhā deula — Temple order characterized by a curvilinear spire which presents the appearance of a continuous line.

Rudra — Terrific form of Śiva.

Śakti — Energy; the supreme power, the creative principle; the goddesses and source existence; spera.

Śaktipiṭha — Centre of Śakti worship, where the corporal remain of goddess Satī is fallen.

Sapta Mātṛkā — The seven divine mothers, the most popular images being Brahmāṇī, Śivānī, Kaumārī, Vaiṣṇavī, Indrāṇī, Vārāhī, and Chāmuṇḍā.

Saptraratha — Temple with seven projections or *pagas* on each side.

Śikhara — Spire of the *rekhā* temple.

Śilpa śāstra — Sanskrit manual giving general principles and rules of architecture and allied arts.

Śilpī — Craftsman.

Siṁha — Lion.

Śiva-*liṅgam* — Phallic emblem of Lord Śiva.

Stambha — Pillar.

Sthānu — Static, immovable.

Sūrya — Sun.

Tala-bandhana — Stringcourse at the base of the *jāṅgha* immediately above the *paga*.

Tāla-jāṅgha — Lower shin.

Tri-ratha — See *ratha*.

Ūpara-jāṅgha — Upper part of shin (thigh).

Ūrdhvabandhana — Stringcourse at the top of the *jāṅgha*.

Ūrdhva-liṅgam — Erect phallus.

Vajra-mastaka — An elaborate double *chaitya*-medalliions crowned by a *kīrttimukha* decorating the *rāhā-pagas* of the *vimāna*.

Vajra-muṇḍī	Miniature shrine with a *vajramastaka* as its crowning element carved as a decorative motif on *pagas* on *jāṅghas.*
Vāstu-puruṣa	Temple is conceived as super human being.
Vāstu Śāstra	Sanskrit texts containing principles regarding building of temples and other religious structures.
Vidyādhara	Supernatural being who flies in the sky, usually carrying a garland; bearer of knowledge.
Vigraha	Image.
Viśvapadma	Lotus seat with petals in both upper and lower directions; double lotus.
Yakṣa/yakṣīṇī	Demi-god associated with fertility, vegetation, female is *yakṣīṇī.*
Yoni	The female organ of generation.

Bibliography

Primary Source

Adhyātma Rāmāyaṇa, Gita Press, Gorakhpur.

Agni Purāṇa, Anandasrama Sanskrit Series, Poona, 1957.

Agni Purāṇa, M.N. Dutta (tr.), Calcutta, 1903-04.

Amara Kośa, Narela Kishore Press, Lahore, 1918.

Aparājita Vāstu Śāstra, Vishvakarma.

Aparājitapṛcchā, Lal Mani Dubey, Laksmi Publications, New Delhi, 1987.

Aparājitapṛcchā: A Critical Study, L.M. Dubey, Allahabad, 1987.

Aṣṭādhyāyī of Pāṇini, S.C. Vasu (ed. and tr.), Allahabad, 1891.

Atharvaveda, S.P.D. Satvalekar (ed.), Bombay, 1938.

Bhāgavata Purāṇa, Gita Press, Gorakhpur.

Bhaviṣya Purāṇa, Venkatesh Press, Bombay, 1910.

Bhuvana Pradīpa, N.K. Bose (ed.), Calcutta, 1929.

Brahma Vaivarta Purāṇa, Guru Mandala Granth Mala and Venkatashwar Press, Bombay, Saṁvat 1988.

Brahmāṇḍa Purāṇa, Venkateshwara Press, Bombay, 1923.

Bṛhadāraṇyaka Upaniṣad, S. Acharya (with commentary), A.S.S. Poone, 1915.

Bṛhaddharma Purāṇa, Chaukhamba Amarabharati Prakashan, Banaras, 1897.

Bṛhat Saṁhitā, Varāha Mihira.

Bṛhat Tantrasāra, Krsnananda Agamavagisa, Navabharat Publishers, Calcutta.

Chaṇḍī Maṅgala, Mukunda Ram, Sukumar Sen (ed.), Calcutta University Publication.

Chaṇḍī Purāṇa, Saral Dasa, Friends Publisher, Cuttack, 1977.

Chaturvarga Cintāmaṇi, Hemadri, Bibliotheca Indica, Calcutta, 1873-1911.

Devī Pūjā, Palm-Leaf Manuscript (Catalogue no. T/74), Orissa State Museum, Bhubaneswar.

Devī Purāṇa, Pancanana (ed.), Bangvasi Press, Calcutta, 1909.

Devī-Bhāgavata Purāṇa, Pandita Pustakalaya, Banaras, 1969.

Devī-Bhagavata, Guru Mandal Series, Calcutta, 1960.

Devī-Māhātmya, V.S. Agrawal, Allahabad, 1963.

Durgāpūjā Paddhati, a palm-leaf manuscript possessed by Mrityunjaya Rath, village Ramesvara, district Khurda.

Durgāsaptaśatī, Swami Jagdishwarananda, Sri Ramakrishna Math, Madras, 1955.

Durgā Tantra Śāstra, Laxmi Narayana Goswami, Dip Publication, Agra, 1997.

Durgā Pūjā Paddhati, a palm-leaf manuscript possessed by Lingaraja Mishra, Village Chandrama Pattapur, district Puri.

Durgāyajanadīpikā, Jagannatha Acharya, a palm-leaf manuscript (Catalogue no. T/5), Orissa State Museum, Bhubaneswar.

Durgotsavacandrikā, a plam-leaf manuscript possessed by Chandrasekhar Samantary, temple Priest of Lord Kapileśvara, Village Dia, district Khurda.

Durgotsavacandrikā, Rama Chandra Gajapati, Palm-Leaf manuscript (Catalogue no. T/82), Orissa State Museum, Bhubaneswar.

Durgotsavacandrikā, Vardhana Mahapatra, Palm-Leaf manuscript (Catalogue no. T/51 and T/81), Orissa State Museum, Bhubaneswar.

Durgotsavapūjā, Palm-Leaf manuscript (Catalogue no. T/100), Orissa State Museum, Bhubaneswar.

Ekāmra Candrikā, R. Gargavatu (ed.), Cuttack, 1931.

Ekāmra Purāṇa, L. Gargavatu (ed.), Cuttack, 1933.

Garuḍa Purāṇa, M.N. Dutt (ed.), Calcutta, 1908; Pansikar (ed.), Bombay, 1924; R.S. Bhattacharya (ed.), Benaras, 1894.

Gautama Dharma Sūtra, L. Srinivasacarya, Mysore, 1917.

Halāyudhakośa, Chaukhambha Sanskrit Series, Banaras.

Harivaṁśa Purāṇa, Ramachandra Shastri (ed.), Oriental Research Institute, Poona, 1936; Gita Press, Gorakhpur.

Hevajra Tantra: A Critical Study, Introduction and translation by D.L. Snellgrove, London, 1959.

Īśāna Śiva Gurudeva Paddhati, T.S.S., Trivandrum, 1920-24.

Jñānārṇava Tantra, Ananda Asrama Series, 1912.

Kālikā Purāṇa, Venkateshwar Press, Bombay, Saṁvat 1964.

Kāmikāgama, MS no. D5431, Government Oriental Manuscript Library, Madras.

Kathāsaritsāgara of Somadeva, C.H. Tawney (tr.), N.M. Penzer (ed.), London, 1924.

Kena Upaniṣad, Bombay, 1927.

Kulacūḍāmaṇi Nigama, Arthur Avalon (ed.), Madras, 1956.

Kaulārṇava Tantra, T.T.S, Calcutta, 1917.

Kulārṇava Tantra, John Woodroffe (ed.), A. Avalon and M.P. Pundit, Madras, 1965.

Kūrma Purāṇa, Guru Mandal Series, Calcutta, 1962.

Liṅga Purāṇa, J.V. Bhattacharya (ed.), Calcutta, 1885; Guru Mandal Series, Calcutta, 1960.

Madalapañjī, A.B. Mohanty (ed.), Utkal University, 1960.

Mahābhārata, Satvaleka (ed.), Ajmavedic Press, 1940; M.N. Dutt (tr.), (Banga Vasi Edition) Calcutta, 1895-1905; P.C. Ray (tr.) (new edition), Calcutta, 1926-32.

Mahānirvāṇa Tantra, Gita Press, Gorakhpur.

Mahānirvāṇa Tantra, John Woodroffe, Madras, 1985.

Mānasāra, P.K. Acharya (ed.), London, 1932.

Mānasollāsa of Bhaṭṭa Someśvara, Mysore, 1926.

Manusmṛti, Choukhamba Sanskrit Series, Benaras, 1935.

Mārkaṇḍeya Purāṇa, V.S. Agrawal, Allahabad, 1961; K.M. Banerjee (ed.), Calcutta, 1862; F.E. Pargiter (tr.), Calcutta, 1904.

Mātṛkā Bheda Tantra, C. Bhattacharya (ed.), Calcutta, 1933.

Matsya Purāṇa, H.N. Apte (ed.), A.S.S., Poona, 1907; H.H. Wilson (tr.).

Meru Tantra, N.S.P., Bombay, 1908.

Muṇḍaka Upaniṣad, Nirnaya Sagara Press, Bombay, 1918.

Nāṭya Śāstra of Bharat Muni, M.M. Ghosh (tr.), Calcutta, 1967.

Nityaṣoḍaśīkārṇava, V.V. Dviveda (ed.) (S.S.V.), Yogatantra Grantha Mala, Banaras, 1905.

Odishara Debadevī, Odisha Book Store, Binodbihari, Cuttack, 1980.

Odishara Śākta Saṁskṛti, Odisha Cultural Forum, 1980.

Padma Purāṇa, Bengal Printing Works, Calcutta, 1959.

Prāchī Māhātmya, Dvija Trilochana, Cuttack, 1898.

Prāṇa Toṣiṇī, Ram Toshana Bhattacharya, Calcutta, 1898.

Prapañcasāra Tantra, A. Avalon (ed.), 1935.

Prapañcasāra Saṅgraha, Govind Chandra Sarasvati.

Prapañcasāratantram, Atalananda Sarasvati (ed.), Motilal Banarsidass, Delhi, 1981.

Raghuvaṁśa, H.D. Valenkar (ed.), Bombay, 1948.

Rāmāyaṇa, J.M. Mehta and others (ed.), Oriental Institute, Baroda, 1960;, N. Ramaratnam (ed.), Madras, 1958.

Ṛgveda Saṁhitā, Ajmer Vedic Press, Saṁvat 1973; Satvalekar (ed.), 1940.

Ṛgveda, N.S. Sontakke and C.G. Kashikar (ed.), Vaidika Saṁsodhana Mandala, Poona, 1933-51.

Rudra Yāmala Tantra, Ramchandra Kak (ed.), Kashmir, 1941.

Rūpamaṇḍana, Balaram Srivastav (ed.), Motilal Banarsidass, Delhi, 1992.

Śabda Kalpa Druma, Chaukhamba Sanskrit Series Varanasi, 1961.

Sādhanamālā, Benoytosh Bhattacharyya (ed.), 2 vols., Baroda, 1968.

Śākta Pramoda, Sri Venkatesvara Press, Bombay, 1951.

Śākta Upaniṣad, A.M. Sastri (ed.), Adyar Library, 1950.

Śakti Aṅka Kalyāṇa, Gita Press, Gorakhpur, 1934.

Śakti Saṅgama Tantra, B. Bhattacharya (ed.), Oriental Institute, Baroda, 1932, 1941, 1947.

Śāradā Tilaka Tantram, A Board of Scholars, Delhi, 1988.

Śāradā Tilakam, Chamanlal Gautam, Barelly, 1985.

Śāradāsaradarcchanā Paddhati, Godavara Mahapatra, a palm-leaf manuscript (Catalogue no. T/13), Orissa State Museum, Bhubaneswar.

Śatapatha Brāhmaṇa, Achuta Grantha Mala, Kashi, S. 1994; Albrecht Weber (ed.), Chaukhamba Sanskrit Series, Banaras, 1964.

Saundaryalaharī, S.S. Sastri (ed.), Adyar, 1937; Oriental Institute, Baroda, 1941.

Śilpa Prakāśa, Rama Chandra Kaulacara, Alice Boner and Sadasiva Ratha Sarma (tr.), Leiden, 1966.

Śilparatna, T.S.S, Trivandrum, 1922.

Śiva Mahā Purāṇa, Nag Publishers, Delhi.

Śiva Purāṇa, A Board of Scholars, Motilal Banarsidass, Delhi, 1970.

Skanda Purāṇa, Guru Mandal Series, Calcutta, 1962.

Skanda Purāṇa, Mansukharaja Mora, Calcutta, 1959-62.

Śilpa Śāstra, Kasyapa, Saraswati Mahal Publications, Tanjore.

Śvetāśvataropaniṣad, Swami Tyagisananda, Sri Ramakrishna math, Mylapore, 1959.

Śyāmārcchanātaraṅgiṇī, A palm-leaf manuscript possessed by Narasimha Mahapatra, Village Maitratrilocanpur, district Puri.

Taittirīya Āraṇyaka, Ananda Asrama Series, Poona, 1967-69.

Taittirīya Brāhmaṇa, Ananda Asrama Series, Poona, 1934-38.

Tantra Yoga, Nik Douglas, Munshiram Manoharlal, New Delhi, 1971.

Tatttirīya Saṁhitā, Ananda Asrama Series, Poona.

The Śākta Upaniṣad, A.G. Krisna Warrier (tr.), Adyar Library and Research Center, Madras, 1964.

The Saundaryalaharī or *Flood of Beauty*, W. Norman Brown (ed. and tr.), Harvard University Press, Cambridge, 1958.

Tripūra Rahasya, Māhātmya Khaṇḍa, Chaukhamba Sanskrit Series, Benaras, Saṁvat 1988.

Vājasaneyī Saṁhitā, Nirnaya Sagara Press, 1928.

Vājasaneyī Saṁhitā, V.L. Shastri Panikhar, Bombay, 1912.

Vāmana Purāṇa, Anand Swarup Gupta (ed.), S.M. Mukhopadhyaya and others (tr.), All India Kashiraj Trust, Banaras, 1968.

Varāha Purāṇa, Gita Press, Gorakhpur; H. Sastri (ed.), Calcutta, 1893.

Vāstu Śāstra, D.N. Shukla, Gorakhpur University, 1958.

Vāyu Purāṇa, R.L. Mitra (ed.), Calcutta 1880-86; M.C. Apte (ed.), A.S.S., Poone, 1905-1907; Venkatesvara Press, Bombay, Saṁvat 1933.

Viṣṇudharamottara Purāṇa, Sri Venkatesvara Press, Bombay, 1938.

Viṣṇu Purāṇa, H.H. Wilson (tr.), Punthi Pustak, Calcutta, 1961.

Viśvakarmāvatāra Śāstra, Trivandrum Sanskrit Series.

Yoginīhṛdaya, Gopinath Kaviraja (ed.), Banaras, 1924.

Secondary Sources

Acharya, K. (1905) "Varieties of Stones used in Building Temples and Making Images in Orissa", *O.H.R.J.*, 13.

——— (1953) "The Commemorative Inscription of the Ananta-Vasudeva Temple Bhubaneswar", *O.H.R.J.*, 1 (4).

——— (1964) "Studies in Temple Architecture in Orissa", *O.H.R.J.*, 12.

Acharya, P. (1953) "Note on the Navagraha Slab in the Temple of Orissa", *O.H.R.J.*, 1: 274-78.

——— (1964) "Studies in Temple Architecture in Orissa", *O.H.R.J.*, 12: 9-12.

——— (1969) *Studies in Orissa History, Archaeology and Archives*, Cuttack.

——— (1974) "The Brahmeśvara Temple Inscription of the Eighteenth Regnal Year of King Udyotakesari", *J.A.S.B.*, 13.

Acharya, P.K. (1918) *Encyclopaedia of Hindu Architecture* (2 vols.), J.K. Publishing House, Bhopal.

Agrawal, P.K. (1969) *Gupta Temple Architecture*, Benaras.

Agrawal, R.C. (1998) *Kashmir and its Monumental Glory*, Aryan Books International, New Delhi.

Agrawala, R.C. (1964) "Ambikā temple at Jagat", *Arts Asiatiques*, 10.

Anonymous (1949?) "Monuments in the Mahānadī Valley", *Orissa Review, Orissa Monuments Special.*

Aryan, Subhashini (1994) *Himadri Temple (AD 700-1300)*, Indian Institute of Advanced Study, Shimla.

Barrett, Douglas E. (1974) *Early Cola Architecture and Sculpture (AD 866-1014)*, Faber, London.

Barett, Douglas and Dikshit, M.G., Mukhalingam (1960) *Sirpur and Rajim Temples*, Bombay.

Beglar, J.D., "Report on Tours in the South-Eastern Provinces in 1874-75 and 1875-76", *ASIR*, 13.

Behera, K.S. (1976) "Brahmanical Temples of Orissa", *Orissa Review* (*Monument Special)*, Bhubaneswar, pp. 55-79.

——— (1993) *Temples of Orissa*, Bhubaneswar.

Bhandarkar, D.R. (1904-05) "The Temple of Narasiṁhanātha", *ASIAR*.

Bhattacharya, T.P. (1986) *The Canons of Indian Art*, Calcutta.

Boner, A., Sarma, Sadasiva Rath and Das, R.P. (1972) *New Light on the Sun Temple of Konarka*, Varanasi.

Bose, N.K. (1932) *Canons of Orissan Architecture*, Calcutta.

Brown, Percy (1965) *Indian Architecture: Buddhist and Hindu Period*, D.B. Taraporewala & Sons, Bombay.

Burgess, J. (1897-1911) *Ancient Monument: Temples and Sculptures of India* (2 vols.), London.

Chakravarti, M.M. (1898) "The Date of the Jagannath Temple in Puri, Orissa", *JASB.*

Chandra, Pramod (ed.) (1975) *Studies in Indian Temple Architecture,* American Institute of Indian Studies, Delhi.

Chhabra, B.Ch., "Ranipur-Jharial Inscriptions", *EI,* 24.

Coomaraswamy, A.K. (1927/2003) *History of Indian and Indonesian Art,* Goldston (reprinted by Kessinger Publishing), London.

Cousens, H. (1897) *List of Antiquarian Remains in the Central Provinces and Berar,* Calcutta, New Imperial Series, no. 19.

——— (1926/1996) *The Calukyan Architecture of the Kanarese Districts,* Archaeological Survey of India, Delhi (reprint).

——— (1985) *Mediaeval Temples of Dakhan,* New Delhi: Cosmo Publications, 1985.

Das, D.R. (1982) *Temples of Orissa: A Study of Sub-Style,* New Delhi.

——— "Kośalesvara Temple at Baidyanātha (Balangir District, Orissa)", *Artibus Asiatique,* 38.

Das, H.C., "Hypaethral Yoginī Temples of Khajurāho and Orissa: A Comparative Study", *O.H.R.J.,* 32 (3 & 4).

Das, M. (1970) *Temples of India,* Bombay.

Das, R.K. (1964) *Temples of Tamilnadu,* Bombay.

Dash, D.R. (1982) *Temples of Orissa: A Study of Sub-style,* New Delhi.

——— (1983) "Stellate Temple of Orissa", In: J. Chakrabarty and D.C. Bhattacharyya (ed.), *Aspects of Indian Art and Culture (S.K. Saraswati Commemoration Volume),* Calcutta.

Dash, M.P. (1962) "Worship of Saptamātṛkās and their Representation in Orissan Temples", *O.H.R.J.,* 11 (2):114-128.

Datta, B.K. (1975) *Bengal Temples,* Munshiram Manoharlal, New Delhi.

Deheja, Vidya (1972) *Early Buddhist Rock Temples,* Cornell University Press, New York.

——— (1979) *Early Stone Temple of Orissa,* New Delhi.

——— (1986) *Yogini Cult and Temples: A Tantric Tradition*, New Delhi.

Deva, Krishna (1969) *Temples of North India*, New Delhi.

——— (2000) *The Temples of North India*, National Book Trust, New Delhi.

Dhaky, M.A. (1998) *Encyclopaedia of Indian Temple Architecture North India, Beginnings of Medieval Indian 900-1000*, New Delhi.

Donaldson, T.E. (1976a) "Development of Gavākṣa Windows in Orissa", *JISOA*, 7: 1-26.

——— (1976b) "Door frames on the earliest Orissan Temples", *A.A.*, 38: 189-219.

——— (1976c) "Development of Vajramastaka on Orissan Temple", *E.W.*, 26: 419-433.

——— (1977) "Decorative Programmes of the Superstructure on the Orissan *Rekha Deula*", In: M.N. Das (ed.), *Side Lights on History of Orissa and Culture*, Cuttack.

——— (1978) "Decorative Scroll Motifs on Orissan Temples", *E.W.*, 28: 225-248.

——— (1983) "Beautiful and Terrifying Śākta Images of Orissa", *Arts of Asia*, 13 (1).

——— (1985-87) *Hindu Temple Art of Orissa* (3 vols.), Leiden.

——— (1988) "Some Little-Known Metal Images from Orissa", *Art of Asia*, 18 (1).

——— (2002) *Tantra and Sakta Art of Orissa* (3 vols.), New Delhi.

——— "Development of the Gavākṣa Window on Orissan Temples", *JISOA*, 7.

Donaldson, T.E. and Behera, K.S. (1988) *Sculpture Masterpieces from Orissa; Style and Iconography*, New Delhi.

Donaldson, T.E. and R.P. Mohapatra (1998) *Ornaments of Orissa*, Delhi.

Encyclopaedia of Indian Temple Architecture (2001) vol. I, part 4a: *South India: Integrated Styles of South India (C.AD 1289-1798)*, Michael W. Meister and M.A. Dhaky (ed.), AIIS, New Delhi.

Encyclopaedia of Indian Temple Architecture (1991) vol. II, part 2: *North India: Period of Early Maturity (C.AD 700-900)*, M.A. Dhaky and Michael W. Meister (ed.), American Institute of Indian Studies, New Delhi.

Encyclopaedia of Indian Temple Architecture (1986) vol. I, part 2: South India: *Upper Dravidadesa Early Phase (AD 550-1075)*, Michael W. Meister and M.A. Dhaky (ed.), AIIS, New Delhi.

Encyclopaedia of Indian Temple Architecture (1983) vol. I, part 1: *South India: Lower Dravidadesa, 200 BC-AD 1324*, Michael W. Meister (ed.), American Institute of Indian Studies, New Delhi.

Encyclopaedia of Indian Temple Architecture (1996) vol. I, part 3: *South India: Upper Dravidadesa: Later Phase (AD 973-1326)*, M.A. Dhaky (ed.), AIIS and IGNCA, New Delhi.

Encyclopaedia of Indian Temple Architecture (1988) vol. II, part 1: *North India: Foundations of North India Style, c.250 BC-AD 1100*, Michael W. Meister, M.A. Dhaky and Krishna Deva (ed.), AIIS, New Delhi.

Encyclopaedia of Indian Temple Architecture (1998) vol. II, part 3: *North India: Beginnings of Medieval Idiom (c. AD 900-1000)*, M.A. Dhaky (ed.), American Institute of Indian Studies, New Delhi.

Fabri, Charles (1974) *History of the Art of Orissa*, Bombay.

Fergusson, J.A. (2001) *A History of Indian and Eastern Architecture*, Munshiram Manoharlal, New Delhi.

Fredric, L. (1959) *Indian Temples and Sculptures*, London.

Ganguly, A. (1954) *Indian Temple Sculptures*, Calcutta.

Ganguly, M.M. (1912) *Orissa and Her Remains*, Calcutta.

George Michell (1975) *An Architectural Description and Analysis of the Early Western Cālukyan Temples*, Art and Archaeology Research Papers, London.

Ghosh, Amalananda (ed.) (1974) *Jaina Art and Architecture* (vol. 1), Bharatiya Jnanapeeth, New Delhi.

Goswami, A. (1959) *Indian Temple Sculptures*, Culcutta.

Gravely, F.H. (1936) *Outline of Indian Temple Architecture*, Madras.

Grover, Satish (2003) (2nd edn.) *Buddhist and Hindu Architecture in India*, CBS Publishers, New Delhi.

Gupte, R.S. (1972) *Iconography of the Hindus, Buddhists and Jains*, Bombay.

——— (1967) *The Art and Architecture of Aihole: A Study of Early Chalukyan Art through Temple Architecture and Sculpture*, D.B. Taraporevala Sons & Co., Bombay.

Havell, E.V. (1911) *Handbook of Indian Art*, London, 1911.

Jayashanker, S. (1997) *Temples of Kerala,* Directorate of Census Operations, Kerala, 1997.

Kak, Subhash (2005) Early Indian Architecture and Art, Migration & Diffusion, An International Journal, vol. 6/Nr.23, 2005, pp.6-27.

Kramrisch, Stella (1981) *Indian Sculptures,* First Indian Reprint, New Delhi.

——— (1947) "The Walls of Orissan Temples", *J.I.S.O.A.*, 15: 178-196.

——— (1954) *The Art of India,* New York.

——— (1946/1996) *The Hindu Temples* (2 vols.), Calcutta, (reprint) Motilal Banarsidass, New Delhi.

Krishna Deva (1974) "Central India: Examples of Ealy Medival Art in Central India", In: A. Ghosh (ed.), *Jaina Art and Architecture,* vol. I, Delhi.

Kuraishi, M.H. (1931) "List of Ancient Monuments protected under Act VII of 1904 in the Province of Bihar and Orissa", *ASI, NIS,* 51.

Lal, Kanwar (1970) *Temples and Sculptures of Bhubaneswar,* New Delhi.

Longhurst, A.H. (1909-10) "Ancient Brick Temples in Central Provinces", *A.S.I.A.R.*, pp. 11-17.

——— (1982) *Pallava Architecture* (3 vols.), Cosmo Publication, New Delhi.

Mahalingam, TV. (1970) *Studies in the South Indian Temple Complex* (Kannada Research Institute Research Lectures, New Series, no. 2), Kannada Research Institute, Karnatak University, Dharwar.

Mahapatra, K.N. (1953) "A Note on the Hypaethral Temple of Sixty-Four Yoginīs at Hirapur", *O.H.R.J.*, 2.

——— (1954) "Gaganaśivācharya and the date of the Monuments at Ranipur-Jharial", *O.H.R.J.*, 2.

Mahapatra, Manamohan (1981) *Traditional Structure and Change in an Orissan Temple,* Calcutta.

Mahtab, H.K. (1959) *The History of Orissa,* 2 vols., Cuttack.

Majumdar, R.C. (ed.) (1957) *The History and Culture of the Indian People,* vol. V, Bombay.

Meister, M.W. (1975) "Jaina Temples in Central India", In: U.P. Shah and M.A. Dhaky (ed.), *Aspects of Jaina Art and Architecture,* Ahmedabad.

——— (1988-89) "Prasada as Palace: Kutina Origins of the Nagara Temple", *Artibus Asiae,* 49 (3/4): 254-280.

Misra, Binayak, "Narasiṁhanātha Stone Inscription of Vaijladeva", *I.H.Q.*, 12.

Mitra, Debala (1960) "Pañca Pāṇḍava Temple of Ganswarpur", *J.N. Banerjea Volume,* Calcutta.

——— (1960) "Four Little-Known *Khākharā* Temples of Orissa, " *J.A.S.B,* 2.

——— (1962) "Archaeological Treasures in Orissa", In: P. Parija and S.C. Mukherji (ed.), *Orissa Past and Present,* Cuttack.

——— (1966) *Bhubaneswar,* Delhi, 1966.

Nath, B.V. (1954) "The Pārvatī Temple Inscription Bhubaneswar", *O.H.R.J.*, 3 (3): 148.

Panda, S.S. (1993) "Some Temple Ruins of Kalahandi District", *O.H.R.J.*, 38 (1-4).

Panigrahi, K.C. (1961) *Archaeological Remains at Bhubaneswar,* Bombay, 1961.

Pargiter, F.E. (1912/1972) *Ancient Indian Historical Tradition,* London, Indian Reprint, New Delhi.

Patel, C.B. (1990) *Dynastic History of Nalas,* Calcutta.

Pathak, V. (1963) *History of Kosala,* Benaras.

Patnaik, J.K. (1998) *Temples of South Kosala (6th century CE-11th century CE): A Case Study of Stellate Temples,* Ph.D. Thesis, Sambalpur University.

Pradhan, B.C. (1983) *Sakti Worship in Orissa,* Ph.D. Dissertation, Sambalpur University.

——— (1996) "Siddheśvara Temple at Palari", Souvenir of *O.H.C* (Silver Jubilee Session), Sambalpur University.

——— (2001) *Rock Art in Orissa,* New Delhi, 2001.

——— (ed.) (2006) *Art and Archaeology of Orissa Recent Perspectives,* New Delhi.

Pradhan, S. (1996) "Siddheśvara Temple at Palari", *Souvenir of O.H.C.* (Silver Jubilee Session), Sambalpur University.

Prasad, B. Rajendra (1983) *Chalukyan Temples of Andhradesa,* Abhinav Publication, New Delhi.

Preston, James J. (1980) *The Cult of the Goddess: Social and Religious Change in a Hindu Temple,* Vikas Publishing House, New Delhi.

Rajan, K.V.S. (1973) *Indian Temple Style,* New Delhi.

Ram Raz (1834) *Essay on the Architecture of the Hindus,* John William Parker, for the Royal Asiatic Society, London.

Rath, B.K., "The Unique Brick Temple at Budhi Komna", In: A.N. Tiwari (ed.), *New Dimension of Tourism in Orissa,* Bhubaneswar.

Sahai, Surendra (2006) *Indian Architecture: Hindu, Buddhist and Jain,* Eastern Book Corporation, Delhi.

Sairam, T.V. (1982) *Indian Temple Forms and Foundation,* New Delhi.

Saraswati, S.K. (1953) "Temple of Orissa", *O.H.R.J.,* 1: 233-253.

Sarker, H. (1978) *An Architectural Survey of Temples of Kerala,* Archaeological Survey of India, New Delhi.

——— (1993) *Studies in Early Buddhist Architecture of India,* Munshiram Manoharlal, Delhi.

Sarma, P.C. (1988) *Architecture of Assam,* Agam Kala Prakashan, Delhi.

Senapati, N. (ed.) (1969) *Orissa District Gazetteers: Balangir,* Cuttack.

——— (ed.) (1971) *Orissa District Gazetteers: Sambalpur,* Cuttack.

Shah, U.P. (1975) "Beginning of the Superstructures in Indian Temple", In: Pramod Chandra (ed.), *Studies in Indian Temple Architecture,* Banaras.

Sharma, D. (1978) *The Temples of Causathi Yogini at Bheraghat,* New Delhi.

Shastri, Ajay-Mitra (1985) "The Date of Lakṣmaṇa Temple at Sirpur", In: F.M. Asher and G.S. Gai (ed.), *Indian Epigraphy : Its Bearing on the History of Art,* New Delhi.

Singh, Harihar (1982) *Jaina Temples of Western India,* Parshvanath Vidyashram Research Institute, Varanasi.

Singhdeo, J.P., "Temples of Nawapara Subdivision", *O.H.R.J.,* 34 (1 & 2).

Sinha, B.P. (1967) "Evolution of Śakti Worship in India", in D.C. Sircar (ed.), *The Sakti Cult and Tara,* Calcutta.

Sinha, A. J. (1996) "Architectural Invention in Sacred Structures: The Case of Vesara Temples of Southern India", *The Journal of the Society of Architectural Historians,* 55 (4): 382-399, Society of Architectural Historians, Chicago.

Sircar, D.C., "A Note on the Latter Somavaṁśīs', *I.H.Q,* 22.

——— (1971) *Religious Life in Ancient and Medieval India,* Delhi.

Sompura, Prabhashankar (1960) *Diparnava* (in Gujarati), Palitana.

Srinivasan, K.R. (1972) *Temples of South India,* National Book Trust, Delhi.

Stadtner, D.M. (1976) *From Sirpur to Rajim (The Art of Kosala During Seventh Century),* Ph.D. Thesis, University of California, Berkeley.

——— (1980) "A Sixth Century A.D. Temple from Kosala", *A.A.A.,* 33: 38-48.

——— (1981) "Siddheśvara Temple at Palari and the Art of Kosala during Seventh-eighth centuries", *Art Orientals,* 12: 49-56.

Stierlin, Henri (2002) *Hindu India: Form Khajuraho to the Temple City of Madurai,* Taschen, Koln.

Stietencron, H.Von (1977) "The Date of Jagannātha Temple Literary Sources Reconsidered", In: M.N. Das (ed.), *Side Lights on History and Culture of Orissa,* Cuttack.

Tadgell, Christopher (1998) *The History of Architecture in India,* Phaidon Press Limited, London.

Thakur, Laxman S. (1996) *The Architectural Heritage of Himachal Pradesh: Origin and Development of Temple Style,* Munshiram Manoharal Publishers, New Delhi.

Tiwari, S.P. (1985) *Comprehensive History of Orissa,* Calcutta.

Tomory, Edith (2006) *A History of Fine Arts in India and the West,* Orient Longman, Chennai.

Trivedi, R.D. (1990) *Temples of the Pratihara Period in Central India,* Archaeological Survey of India, New Delhi.

Vasu, N.N. (1981) *The Archaeological Survey of Mayurbhanja,* Delhi.

Vats, M.S. (1951) "The Gupta Temple at Deogarh", *M.A.S.I.*, 70.

Wave, C.S. (1988) *Serpent Worship and Other Races*, London.

Weiner Shelia (1962) "From Gupta to Pāla Sculpture", *A.A.*, 24: 167-182.

Yazdani, G. (1952) *History of Deccan*, vol. I, London.

Zannas, Eliky S. (1960) *Kharaho*, The Hague.

Zimmer, H. (1962) *Myths and Symbols in Indian Art and Civilization*, New York.

Journals

Annual Reports of the Archeological Survey of India, Ancient India, Bulletin of the Archaeological Survey of India, New Delhi.

Asiatique Researches, Calcutta.

Bharati (Utkal University Research Journal), Bhubaneswar.

Bharati, A Bulletin of the Banaras Hindu University, Varanasi.

Bulletin of the School of Oriental Studies, London.

Chandi (Hindi), Allahabad, 1980-90.

Epigraphica Indica (Government of India Publication), New Delhi.

Indian Antiquary, Bombay.

Indian Culture, Calcutta.

Indian Historical Quarterly, Calcutta.

Jhankara (Odiyā), vol. 37, 1985.

Journal of Ancient Indian History, Calcutta.

Journal of Ancient Indian History, Trivandrum.

Journal of Ancient Society of Bengal (letters), Calcutta.

Journal of Ancient Society of Bengal, Calcutta.

Journal of Andhra Pradesh Historical Research Society, Rajmahendry.

Journal of Andhra the Historical Research Society.

Journal of Asiatic Society, Calcutta.

Journal of Bihar and Orissa Research Society, Bombay.

Journal of Bihar Research Society, Patna.

Journal of Kalinga Historical Research Society, Bolangir.

Journal of New Aspects on History of Orissa, P.G. Dept. History Sambalpur University.

Journal of Numismatic Society of India, Bombay.

Journal of Oriental Research, Madras.

Journal of Royal Society of Arts, London.

Kalyana (Hindi), Gita Press, Gorakhpur, 1987.

Kosala through the Ages (Pamphlet no. 2), Bolangir, 1947.

Memoirs of the Archaeological Survey of India, New Delhi.

New Aspects on History of Orissa, P.G. Dept. of History, Sambalpur University.

Nirmalya (Oriyā), Kacheri Road, Puri, issues from 1993-1995.

Orissa Historical Research Journal, Bhubaneswar.

Orissa Review, (Relevant issues).

Prachya Pratibha, Bhopal.

Proceedings of Indian History Congress, (Published from different places).

Saptarsi, Sambalpur University Journal.

Satayarsiki Smaranika, Sahitya Samiti, Khariar, 1983.

Srimandira (Oriyā), Jagannath Mission, Puri, issues from 1990-1995

The Heritage, December, 1986.

The Konark, vol. 36, 1978, vol. 39, 1979.

The Mirror, vol. X, no. 1, November, 1970.

Utkala Prasanga (Odiyā).

Vijaya (Oriyā), Madras and Bhubaneswar, November 1995.

Gazetteers

Behuria, N.C., *Orissa State Gazetteer*, Orissa State, 3 vols., 1990-91

Bhatta, S.C. (ed.), *The Encyclopaedic District Gazetteers of India, Eastern Zone*, vol. 9, New Delhi, 1997.

Senapati, N. and D.C. Kumar, *Puri District Gazetteers*, Cuttack, 1977.

Senapati, N. (ed.), *Orissa District Gazetteers*, Bolangir, 1968.

——— (ed.), *Baudh Kandhmal District Gazetteers*, Cuttack, 1983.

——— (ed.), *Bolangir District Gazetteers*, Cuttack, 1968.

——— (ed.), *Kalahandi District Gazetteers*, Cuttack, 1980.

——— (ed.), *Sambalpur District Gazetteers*, Cuttack, 1971.

——— (ed.), *Koraput District Gazetteers*, Cuttack, 1966.

——— (ed.), *Sundargarh District Gazetteers*, Cuttack, 1975.

Verma, Rajendra (ed.), *Madhya Pradesh District Gazetteers* (Relevant volumes), Bhopal, 1973.

Index

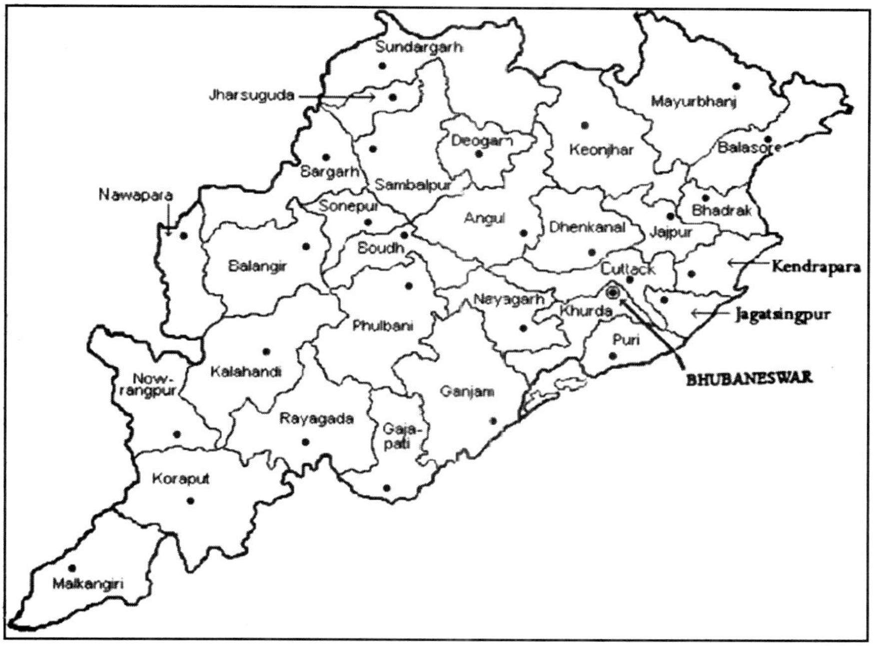

Map 1. Map showing the location of modern districts

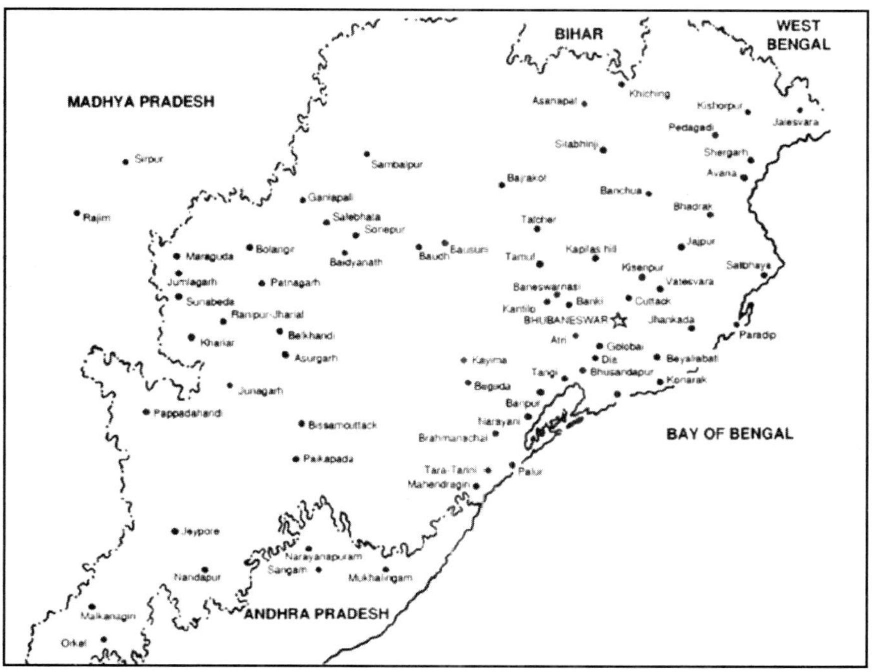

Map 2. Map showing the major Śākta shrines and *khākharā* temples

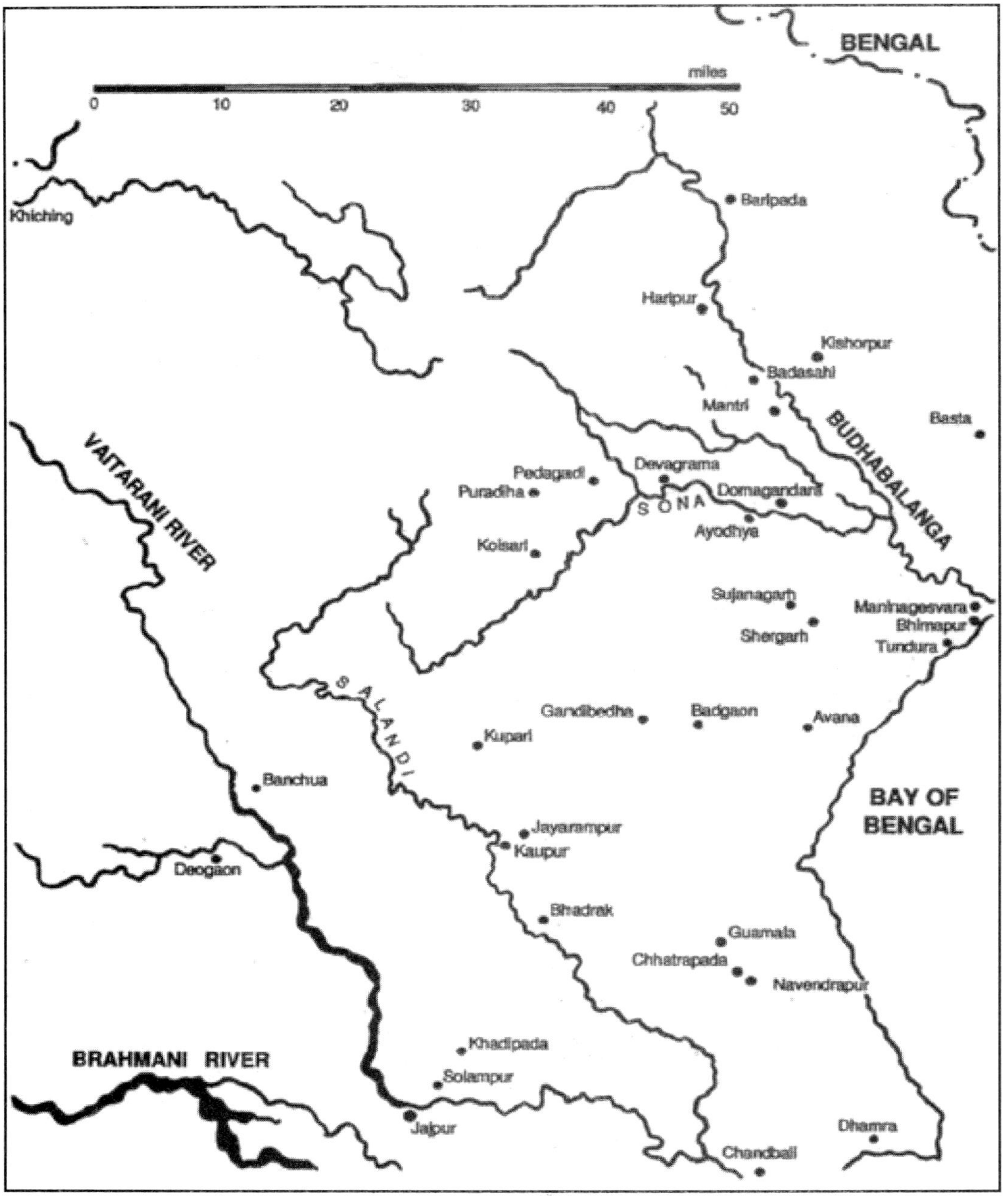

Map 3. Map of north-eastern Orissa showing the prominent Śākta shrines and *khākharā* temples

Map 4. Map of Upper Mahānadī Valley showing the preminent Śākta shrines and *khākharā* temples

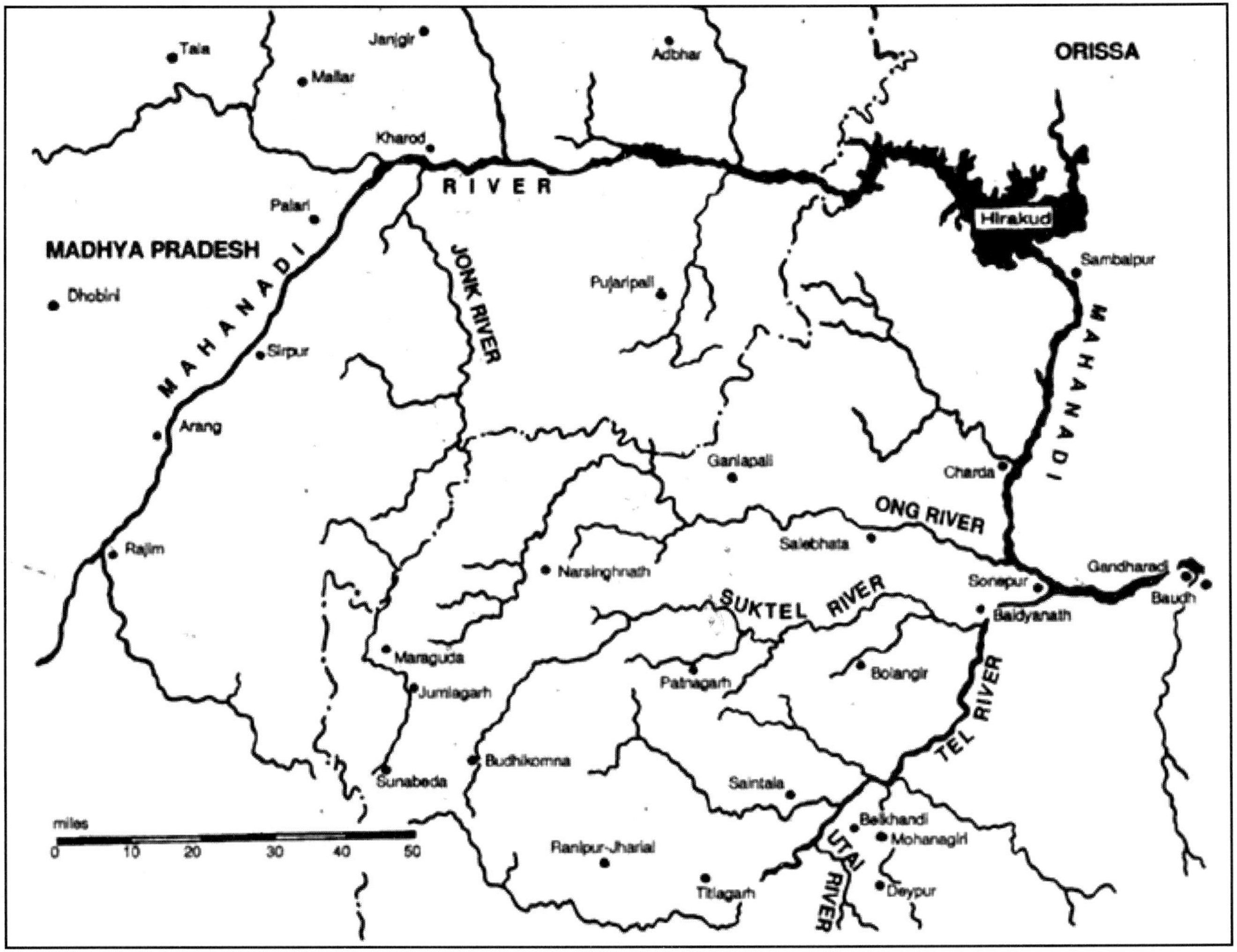

Map 5. Map of the Mahānadī Delta showing the Major Śākta shrines and *khākharā* temples

1. General view of Vaital temple,
Bhubaneswar, Khurda

2. Side view of Vaital temple,
Bhubaneswar, Khurda

3. *Mastaka* of Vaital temple, Bhubaneswar, Khurda

4. Mahiṣamardinī image of Vaital temple, Bhubaneswar, Khurda

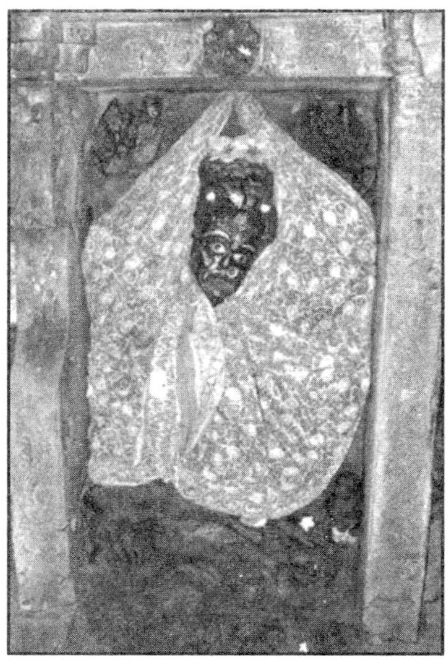

5. Chāmuṇḍā of Vaital temple, Bhubaneswar, Khurda

6. General view of Durgā temple, Baideswar, Cuttack

7. Side view of Durgā temple, Baideswar, Cuttack

8. *Andhakāsura-vadha* image of Durgā temple, Baideswar, Cuttack

9. Mahiṣamardinī image of Durgā temple, Baideswar, Cuttack

10. Mahākālī, Mahālakṣmī and Mahāsarasvatī of Nārāyaṇī temple, Dia, Khurda

11. Chāmuṇḍā image of Nārāyaṇī temple, Dia, Khurda

12. Vaiṣṇavī image of Nārāyaṇī temple, Dia, Khurda

8. *Andhakāsura-vadha* image of Durgā temple, Baideswar, Cuttack

9. Mahiṣamardinī image of Durgā temple, Baideswar, Cuttack

10. Mahākālī, Mahālakṣmī and Mahāsarasvatī of Nārāyaṇī temple, Dia, Khurda

11. Chāmuṇḍā image of Nārāyaṇī temple, Dia, Khurda

12. Vaiṣṇavī image of Nārāyaṇī temple, Dia, Khurda

13. Mahiṣamardinī image of Nārāyaṇī temple, Dia, Khurda

14. General view of Durgā temple, Sergarh, Balasore

15. Mahiṣamardinī image of Durgā temple, Sergarh, Balasore

16. General view of Nārāyaṇī temple, Chilika, Ganjam

17. *Mastaka* of Nārāyaṇī temple, Chilika, Ganjam

18. Mahiṣamardinī image of Nārāyaṇī temple, Chilika, Ganjam

19. General view of Gaurī temple, Bhubaneswar, Khurda

20. General view of Vārāhī temple, Chaurasi, Puri

21. *Mastaka* of Vārāhī temple, Chaurasi, Puri

22. Vārāhī deity of Vārāhī temple, Chaurasi, Puri

23. General view of Akhadachaṇḍī temple, Bhubaneswar, Khurda

24. Mahiṣamardinī image of Akhadachaṇḍī temple, Bhubaneswar, Khurda

25. *Khākharā* temple inside the Mukteśvara temple compound, Bhubaneswar, Khurda

26. Smaller *khākharā* temple, Ranipur-Jharial, Bolangir

27. General view of Gopāliṇī temple inside Liṅgarāja temple, Bhubaneswar, Khurda

28. General view of Sāvitrī temple inside Liṅgarāja temple, Bhubaneswar, Khurda

29. General view of Vārāhī temple inside Liṅgarāja temple, Bhubaneswar, Khurda

30. Vārāhī image of Vārāhī temple inside Liṅgarāja temple, Bhubaneswar, Khurda

31. General view of Dakṣiṇachaṇḍī temple, Hadapada, Khurda

32. Mahiṣamardinī deity of Dakṣiṇachaṇḍī temple, Hadapada, Khurda

33. Kālī image in the temple complex of Dakṣiṇachaṇḍī temple, Hadapada, Khurda

34. Chhinamastā image in the temple complex of Dakṣiṇachaṇḍī temple, Hadapada, Khurda

35. General view of Gaṅgeśvarī temple, Bayalisbati, Puri

38. Mahiṣamardinī, presiding deity of Gaṅgeśvarī temple, Bayalisbati, Puri

36. Mahiṣamardinī image of Gaṅgeśvarī temple, Bayalisbati, Puri

37. *Mastaka* of Gaṅgeśvarī temple, Bayalisbati, Puri